Thirteen *is* a Lucky Number

The Campbell Family

Thirteen *is* a Lucky Number
The Campbell Family

by Trudy Chambers Price

SALT PONDS PRESS
A division of Islandport Press

YARMOUTH • FRENCHBORO • MAINE

Salt Ponds Press
P.O. Box 10
Yarmouth, Maine 04096
saltponds@islandportpress.com
www.islandportpress.com

ISBN: 1-934031-00-3
Library of Congress Control Number: 2006904326

First Edition Published June 2006

Book design by Salt Ponds Press
Cover design by Karen F. Hoots / Mad Hooter Design
Cover photo courtesy of Mary and Bob Campbell
Interior photos courtesy of the Campbell family

Dedication

To Sis
May 15, 1929–March 15, 2006

Contents

Foreword

Bob O'Brien

I met Toni on November 15, 1996, and shortly thereafter, we started visiting her mother in Aroostook County. Her mother was hospitalized in March 1997 and we burned up Interstate 95 to visit Mémère in Cary Medical Center. It was on this visit to Caribou that I met the first Campbell girl, Barbara, [Toni's niece] in Mémère's hospital room.

Mémère Guerrette was the finest lady I ever met in my life. We lost our matriarch. She left some legacies.

Toni told me of her sister Mary and husband Bob, who had a large family, numbering 13 children—a large number for families in the United States today.

During that same trip, Toni wanted dinner at the famed Yusef's Restaurant in Caribou. Upon entering the lobby, we found three nice-looking chicks (young compared to Toni and me) with great smiles. They were out for the evening without husbands and children. Two of these girls were Campbells, Janet and Joan. So, now I had met three Campbell children and only had ten to go.

I then met David at the Presque Isle Fair, then Pat at Mary's M & D Monogramming. I met Sue when Toni and I were invited to a turkey feed at Bob and Mary's; Gary at Christmas mass in Fort

Fairfield; Kim, also. I met Roberta from Atlanta, Georgia, when Mary and about six of her girls came to our Ogunquit home that next spring on a trip to southern Maine. I bought this large horde of women pizzas and volumes of Chinese food, and they well enjoyed it.

I met Sharon leaving mass at Holy Rosary in Caribou; Roger when Mémère was too old and feeble to live alone, and we moved the contents of her apartment from Lyndon Heights to homes of various family members.

Mike and I met at our Ogunquit home at Christmas, and his wife Mary sang songs for Mémère and the rest of us.

I now had only Jim to go. During Potato Blossom Festival in Fort Fairfield, there were pontoon boats to ride on the Aroostook River. Toni and I bought tickets and walked down the ramp to the boat, and the person on the boat called, Hi, Toni. It was Jim and his wife, also named Toni. I finally had found the elusive Jim and shook his hand and called him Number 13. He looked quizzically at this greeting, so I explained he was the last of the Campbells I had been waiting to meet. It was now July 2001.

For the next year or so, I attended some Campbell family functions (large, always) and employed Wayne, Mark, Ben, Andy, and Ann [family members]. I was eager for stories of Aroostook County life. I was born in Boston, and had moved to southern Maine in 1971. I learned of lobstering, musseling, and harpooning giant bluefish tuna out of Perkins Cove, Ogunquit.

I had visited The County in July 1995 on a trip to The Gaspé Peninsula by the St. Lawrence River. The rolling green hills of The County were much different scenery than coastal rockbound Maine. I had spent summers at Wells Beach. I liked the County people, their way of life, and a standard of living that omitted the rat-race style of southern Maine. I sold my vacation home and bought the log home in Fort Fairfield only two months later.

As the stories about Bob and Mary's potato farming in their younger years were told to me, I began to think that there was more subject matter for a book about this family than that of books I had read and documentaries I had seen on TV. I thought the work ethics of potato farming; their later running of the AG store in Easton; the barn burning down, resulting in the loss of all the equipment; and Bob and Mary winning the lottery were more than enough material for a book about Bob, Mary, 13 children, and years of Aroostook County life. So, I began to look for an author for the project. Wayne Troicke [Pat's husband] was attending UMPI (University of Maine at Presque Isle) for two years and was gardening for me summers at the Fort Fairfield house. I asked Wayne to keep his eyes focused for a top student in English literature who would undertake the project— to no avail. While I waited, the project grew in my mind.

My dream of finding an author came true in May 2005 when I met Trudy Price. I had so enjoyed her book, *The Cows Are Out!*, a memoir about 23 years on a Maine dairy farm. I finally have the right person for this project.

Bob O'Brien
September 2005
Fort Fairfield, Maine

Author's Note

Several years ago, my high school friend Toni (Antoinette Guerrette Phillips) introduced Bob O'Brien to her sister Mary, her husband Bob Campbell, and their family. After getting to know them, Bob O'Brien had a dream of preserving their history, stories, and photographs in a book. The dream perked for five years and now, thanks to Toni's suggestion of asking me to be the author, and Bob's generous support, it is a reality.

On May 15, 2005, I met more than 30 of over 60 members of the Campbell family for breakfast at the Village Restaurant in Fort Fairfield, Maine. As soon as I walked into the room, I knew this project would be a big one in many ways. After breakfast, Bob Campbell headed out in his motorized wheelchair. Toni and I wanted to get a picture of him coming up over Fort Hill Street to his house, but by the time we got there, he was settled into the dining room, waiting for us.

Mary was in Bangor with her granddaughter and great-granddaughter to help with the baby's medical appointment. Some other family members gathered there, too. I have never been in a room filled with so much love and laughter. The stories flew left and right! Sherrill immediately informed me that she is the favorite daughter-in-law. I later learned that others claim the same title.

I was overwhelmed that afternoon, but also glad that mostly everyone joined in conversation, storytelling, joking, and teasing. Some even brought photographs.

I finally met Mary in June and got to see the Campbell family photo. It included all thirteen children and would become the cover of the book.

Thirteen *is* a Lucky Number

Trudy and Mary choose photos for the book

After I sent letters to family members and friends asking for their contributions to the book, now with a working title, *Thirteen* is *a Lucky Number*, the e-mails and letters began to arrive.

I traveled upcountry in July for Potato Blossom Festival week to meet with Mary and Bob. During the week, I met 9 of their 13 children, interviewed as many as I could, and tape-recorded their stories. I found that because they are so used to being together as a family, most felt more comfortable being interviewed with at least two or three other family members present. That way they could chime in when the story was also theirs.

When I got to Sharon's house, there must have been 25 people having supper. I was invited to join them, but I had eaten. Sisters were changing and feeding each other's babies. Two dogs and a cat made their presence known. Two cousins were boxing in the back room. The phone rang for various people, and the men went back to their work in the garage. Sharon's girls cleaned up the kitchen and served strawberry shortcake. I remarked on how good the biscuits were.

Straight from KFC, Sharon said.

While I was primarily there to hear Sharon's stories, everyone added anecdotes. Brent teased Lori, You were a mistake.

No, she said, I'm a miracle!

While I was transcribing the tapes to my computer, I recalled the writing style of Kent Haruf in two of his novels that I had just read. After I had read a couple of chapters of *Plainsong*, I wondered how he wrote with such clean flow. Then I realized that besides the fine craft of his writing, it was also because there were no quotation marks in either of his two novels. I liked the style a lot, so I decided that it would work for this book, too.

It was hard work transcribing the tapes, but it put me in touch again with the voices, the lingo, and the enthusiasm of a family that I now feel a part of. I have tried to keep each person's voice as true as possible. I feel more like a story-gatherer than an author because the people in this book are really the authors of their own stories.

I traveled to The County once a month for six months to gather more stories and photographs. I saw potato planting, potato blossoms, potato harvest, and even snow! All of it reinforced my childhood roots, but reconnecting with the County people, and meeting new ones, especially Mary and Bob, has been the best part of all.

Mary and Bob celebrated their 50th wedding anniversary in 2006.

Congratulations!

Trudy Chambers Price
May 2006
Brunswick, Maine

Introduction

There is a clock in the kitchen at the Campbell house that plays the Campbell Soup song every hour on the hour. We all know it. We've all heard it: M'm m'm good! M'm m'm good! That's what Campbell's Soups are! M'm m'm good!

I remarked about it as I interviewed Bob and Mary for the first time. It was a gift. They are so used to it, they don't even hear it anymore. They think it is turned off at night, but they're not sure.

Of course, there are different ways to pronounce the name Campbell. In the song, it goes more like, M'm m'm good! M'm m'm good! That's what Cambull's Soups are! M'm m'm good! making the "p" silent in "Camp" and sounding "bell" as "bull".

This is when Bob said to me, I was born a *Camp-Bell*! I wasn't born a *Cambull*. When I die, I want to die as a *Camp-Bell*. That's who I am.

As I got to know Bob Camp-Bell over this past year, that became his mantra. He knows who he is! He has a strong philosophy on life that you will read about in the son-in-law talk, which he gives to each new young man entering the family. You will find out that Bob is opinionated and isn't afraid to express his thoughts. He goes after what he believes is his, which you will discover when you read his sugar beet story.

All along, Bob has been the prominent storyteller. Mary is quiet. She listened, filled in the blanks, added facts (like which child was born when!), figures, dates, and details. But many times, her one-line zingers at the end of certain stories offer the reader the last laugh.

Thirteen *is* a Lucky Number

The Campbell family likes to be together, so getting individuals alone for interviews was a challenge. Nine of the 13 siblings live in The County, so I was able to meet them in a family setting, where they could chime in on any given story. What fun it was for siblings to hear stories about each other for the first time.

I interviewed three more siblings by phone. Other stories were sent to me in letters and by e-mail. It seemed natural to begin with Mary and Bob, followed by stories told by the children in order of their birth, starting with Sharon and ending with Kim. Now, because Kim, being the youngest and number 13, felt left out of a lot of the sibling stories, let me say to her, Kim, the title of the book, *Thirteen is a Lucky Number!* is really about you!

The last part of the book is devoted to relatives and friends who have anecdotes and special memories of the Campbell family to share.

When I began this writing project, I knew very little about the Campbell family, except that Mary and Bob had 13 children in 14 years and that they had been potato farmers for 18 years. I traveled to The County once a month for six months to gather as much information as I could. Each time I went, I was amazed by the next story, and the next—for example: the fire that burned the huge Ashby barn and its contents to the ground; that Mary had been hit by lightning when she was seven months pregnant with Joan; that they had won the Megabucks; that Bob had a stroke in Boston on 9/11; the plane crash on their farm; Roger's trip across the Atlantic by ship that would change his life; Michael and Mary Nightingale's touching love story; that even though the children are grown, they still gather for a family breakfast every other month.

I have been at some of those breakfasts. After one of them, the children went to their homes and brought photo albums back to Bob and Mary's house to peruse and make choices to be included in the book. I will never forget them scattered everywhere, on the floor, on the porch, enjoying being together. Of course, this is what pleases Mary the most, is to have them all under one roof again.

The themes that show up time and time again in the stories are: The County, the work ethic learned there, the little house, the campground, Pete the ice cream truck, and the five little girls, and the fun!

Everyone has fascinating family history but rarely is it written or recorded in some fashion for future generations.

Here is a glimpse of one family—the Campbells—who are deeply rooted in their small community of Fort Fairfield in Aroostook County, Maine.

~*Trudy Chambers Price*

Part 1
Genealogy

CHAPTER ONE

Genealogy

FAMILY OF:

Mary and Robert Campbell	Date & Place of Birth
Marie Martha Albert Campbell	1/22/39 Sinclair, ME
Robert Louis Campbell (husband)	3/15/37 Caribou, ME
Sharon Marie Campbell Perreault	5/23/56 Torrington, CT
Terry Gene Perreault (husband)	6/28/55 Caribou, ME
Jennifer Jo Perreault	8/27/75 Caribou, ME
Jacob Christopher Dougherty	7/20/96 Presque Isle, ME
Jessica Rose Perreault	5/12/77 Caribou, ME
Travis Wade Robbins (husband)	8/28/74 Presque Isle, ME
Abbigail Ann Robbins	10/10/02 Presque Isle, ME
Jada Rose Robbins	10/20/03 Bangor, ME
Tina Marie Perreault Moir	3/23/79 Caribou, ME
Luke Eric Moir (husband)	5/8/80 Caribou, ME
Emily Lynn Moir	2/24/05 Caribou, ME
Brent Richard Perreault	6/17/80 Caribou, ME
Lori Lynn Perreault Leavitt	8/23/81 Caribou, ME
Randy Lee Leavitt (husband)	12/1/78 Caribou, ME

Patricia Ann Campbell Troicke 7/22/57 Caribou, ME
Wayne Edward Troicke (husband) 12/9/54 Binghamton, NY
    Andrew Martin Troicke 8/28/80 Loring AFB, ME
    Benjamin Wayne Troicke 6/26/82 Loring AFB, ME
    Ann Nicole Troicke 10/3/84 Wichita Falls, TX
        (Sheppard AFB)

Roger John Campbell 9/9/58 Caribou, ME
Doreen Ketch Levasseur Campbell
(1st wife) 10/11/51 Caribou, ME
    Kurt Lee Levasseur (stepson) 10/6/74
    Herbert Wayne Levasseur (stepson) 9/25/76
April McIsaac Campbell (wife) 4/12/59 Caribou, ME

Barbara Jean Campbell Turner 11/12/59 Caribou, ME
David Earl Wark (1st husband) 2/12/57 Caribou, ME
Stuart Turner (husband) 7/11/61 Ft. Fairfield, ME
    Jason David Wark 4/16/80 Caribou, ME
    Janelle Rae Wark 6/4/81 Caribou, ME
    Lance Gustaf Zeigler (husband) 4/10/74 Caribou, ME
        Madison Rae Zeigler 6/15/03 Caribou, ME

David Wayne Campbell 1/18/61 Caribou, ME
Sherrill McKenney Campbell (wife) 9/23/63 Caribou, ME
    Daniel Allen Campbell 10/15/85 Caribou, ME
    Bradley Adam Campbell 6/19/87 Caribou, ME

Gary Alan Campbell   1/15/62 Caribou, ME
Bernice Riley Campbell (1st wife)
    Jessica Marie Riley   9/29/84 Kittery, ME
    Jake Albert Dionne   12/31/82 Caribou, ME
       Trevar Joseph Dionne   3/24/06 Caribou, ME
    Anthony Scott Campbell   12/13/86 Caribou, ME
    Alan Dean Campbell   6/13/88 Caribou, ME
Lisa Marie Beaulieu (wife)   9/9/66 Caribou, ME
    Amanda Marie Campbell   9/29/20 Presque Isle, ME

Michael Paul Campbell   3/3/63 Caribou, ME
Mary Margaret Nightingale Campbell (wife) 3/11/65 Ft. Fairfield, ME
    Zachary Stephen Adams (stepson)   6/8/88 Bangor, ME
    Saré Elizabeth Campbell   5/1/99 Wolfboro, NH

James Robert Campbell   6/1/64 Caribou, ME
Toni Kathleen Fletcher Campbell (wife)   8/1/66 Mars Hill, ME
    Ethan Richard Campbell   10/11/91 Presque Isle, ME

Susan Francis Campbell Cyr   8/18/65 Caribou, ME
Chester Paul Cyr (husband)   2/8/62
    Thomas Matthew Cyr   4/14/87 Bristol, CT
    Jordan Elizabeth Cyr   8/14/88 Bristol, CT
    Kaitlin Marie Cyr   1/25/90 Biddeford, ME

Roberta Louise Campbell Lasater   9/3/66 Caribou, ME
David Lasater (husband)   7/14/66 Sacramento, CA
    Brandon David Lasater   10/9/92 Warner Robbins, GA
    Zachary Taylor Lasater   5/6/95 Warner Robbins, GA
    Spencer Robert Lasater   6/18/00 Warner Robbins, GA

Thirteen *is* a Lucky Number

Joan Marie Campbell Bernard	11/2/67 Caribou, ME
Sean Bernard (husband)	12/9/66 Ft. Fairfield, ME
Noah Michael Bernard	5/2/96 Caribou, ME
Jonathan Lee Bernard	5/28/99 Presque Isle, ME
Janet Helen Campbell Giberson	12/23/68 Caribou, ME
Mark Giberson (husband)	8/14/65 Presque Isle, ME
Nicole Lynn Giberson	5/30/96 Presque Isle, ME
Kayla Elizabeth Giberson	2/14/98 Presque Isle, ME
Christopher Mark Giberson	4/16/99 Presque Isle, ME
Kimberly Ann Campbell Senal	3/12/70 Caribou, ME
Kevin Brian Senal (husband)	9/23/78 Aurora, CO
Blake Alexander Senal	6/19/05 Caribou, ME

Part II
Family

CHAPTER TWO

Elizabeth (Sis) Campbell Matson

*I couldn't wait until Rob was five years old and could help
me pick potatoes. He got to use the child-size potato basket I
used when I started picking at five years of age.*
~ *Sis, Bob's sister*

My father, John W. R. (Wendell Rice) Campbell, bought the
farm on the East Presque Road in 1916. In October of 1917, he and
my mother Elizabeth Helen McGlinn were married. They celebrated
63 years of married life until my mother died in 1980. My father
died three years later.

The first child of John and Lizzie, a boy, died at birth without
being named. Then there was Aloysius. He died at four years of age.
Then Joan died at 18 months. My brother Roland was to follow, and
then I was born 14 months later.

Roland and I named Rob. We were in the third grade at Holy
Rosary School when he was born. We were reading Robert Louis
Stevenson poems and were very impressed with them, so told Mom
his name should be Robert Louis Stevenson. She said she thought it
would be a good idea to drop the Stevenson, but that Robert Louis
could be his name.

Bob, Roland, Lucky and Sis

Roland and I were in the same grade. Roland was a year older and had to go to kindergarten his first year. They dropped kindergarten the following year, so I went into first grade with Roland.

When I was five years old, Charles was born, but lived only seven days. When I was eight years old, Robert was born. When I was 12 years old another baby, a girl, died at birth without being named.

Whenever anyone asked if Rob was the baby of the family, Rob would say, No, I'm not the baby of the flamily, Sally is.

On his own, he named the baby Sally. Instead of family, he would say *flamily*.

Toys weren't in abundance in those days. My only doll was one that Mom had when she was young. It had a cloth stuffed body, and molded hair and eyes.

Bob, Sis and Roland

Sis and Bob (in his Roy Rogers pants)

Rob became my doll. We have always been very close. One upset was when he was about one and a half years old and I had received a doll for Christmas with real hair. He broke off one of her legs. Though she had real hair and eyes that opened and closed, she lived with only one leg.

Roland and I used to push Rob around in a big old baby carriage. We had a pony, Beauty, who was old and slow. Rob used to sit under her in the shade.

I couldn't wait 'til Rob was five years old and could help me pick potatoes. He got to use the child-size potato basket I used when I started picking at five years of age.

Rob and Mary married in 1956. Mary has been a treasure in our family. Sam Matson and I married in 1967. I had been living in

b: Bob, Sis, Evelyn and Roland
f: Lizzie, holding Lona, and John

Bob's confirmation, with Father Albert Cyr and Bishop Feeney

Hannah Mulherne Campbell
[Bob's paternal great-grandmother]

Connecticut for seven years before marriage. I lived with Roland, his wife Evelyn, and their four children: Lona, Wendell, Joseph, and Theresa. Roland later divorced and married Steffie, and had one son named James Vincent.

Roland died in 2000.

I was always very fond of children and enjoyed Roland's while I lived with them. I worked in an office during that time. Whenever we went to Maine, Sam and I always felt Rob's kids were our kids. We had no children, so after seven years, we adopted a son; then another son, and then a daughter. Our boys Ken and Don were the same ages as Mike and Jim, Rob's youngest boys. Our daughter was the same age as one of the five little girls as they were known: Sue, Roberta, Joan, Janet, and Kim. Actually, Roberta and our Marji are the same age.

Aloysius smoking his corncob pipe

14

John and Nancy Sullivan McGlinn
[Bob's maternal great-grandparents]

John M. Campbell and Cecelia Hourihan Campbell
[Bob's paternal grandparents]

We used to take pictures of Rob's kids each year until we had our own. The last picture taken of the group had Mike as a baby. Each year on picture-taking day, Mary would take the oldest, down

b: Freeland Smith, Charles Sullivan, John and Nancy McGlinn
f: Donald Smith

to the youngest, and wash them up, put on fresh clothes, comb their hair, and send them out to sit on Grampy's bench to wait for the big moment. At that time, they lived in the little house on Dad's farm.

There were good times visiting them on the Ashby farm where they moved when they outgrew the little house. Our boys stayed with them there one summer for about two weeks. Our daughter visited with them one summer for about a month after they had moved to the home in Fort Fairfield.

One remembrance was when Dave was about four years old. I happened to go into the cellar and there was Dave, all by himself, lighting broom straws through a slot in the gas furnace where you could see the flames. I told him I thought he should tell his mother and father before he lit any more. He did not grow up to be an arsonist.

One time when Pat was about three years of age, she decided that she was Sam's girl. She followed him everywhere. We had

16

noticed that she had started carrying a folded brown paper grocery bag under her arm wherever she went. We didn't realize until we were ready to leave that she thought she was going with us, and she had a pair of panties in the bag so she would be ready. When she couldn't go, she went behind the porch door and cried and wouldn't say goodbye to us. That was sad.

People would ask how the kids minded so well and Rob would say, I sic Pat on them.

Sharon always tended the babies and Pat took care of the older ones. I once asked Mary how she did it and why the kids were so good.

She said, My first three were a constant care. They were the hardest.

She always had a constant pile of clothes to be washed and ironed and put away. She was some worker.

Rob once said he was visiting someone who had company and she was complaining that she was feeding 10 people three times a day. Rob told her, Try 15 for three meals a day for 365 days a year.

Sis and Sam

17

John standing and Bob driving the 1929 Farmall Regular

She thought about it and decided she was complaining needlessly.

We still enjoy our visits with them. The kids are close to each other and to Rob and Mary. We now enjoy their visits with their kids and now the great-grands are coming along.

It is a wonderful family.

CHAPTER THREE

The Early Years

They were so Irish and I was a French girl.
~Mary

BOB: Mary and I met at Caribou High School. She was a junior and I was a senior. She was in the Future Homemakers of America [FHA], and I was in Future Farmers of America [FFA]. We had combined dances to get together.

MARY: It was ironic. I'm such a bad math person, and he does everything in his head.

Every morning I'd do his bookkeeping homework. He didn't do his homework. He aced it and so did I.

BOB: I worked for Dad after I graduated. I worked on the freezer plant at the Birds Eye building. We were tarring the top and I fell off, got burnt and was laid up for two or three months before I went to Connecticut.

Mary and I were married at Holy Rosary Catholic Church in Caribou, February 6, 1956. We met the priest in the basement for rehearsal.

The church wasn't finished yet—it burnt down. We had Father Grondin. He was just a new priest and he went through the things. He says, Well, I don't know. I know some people got married last week. We were glad, so if they answered the questions this way, it's the way it should be. If they said yes, then we should say yes.

Father Cyr married us. We had breakfast at my mother's and father's. That was our big time. That was our reception. Next year will be 50 years. We stayed at Mom and Dad's that night. Then we took off next day for Connecticut. Got to Bangor. Well, no, we got to Old Town. Then it took to snowing so hard. Cars were all off the road everywhere. We were something like two hours getting to Bangor. Started up Hammond Street hill. Had a great big Chrysler Imperial car. Got pretty near to the top and couldn't make it. A guy came along with a little VW with chains on. Hit me right in the ass, and took me right up over the hill. Made his day. Then we started down the other side, and the Queen City Motel is through there, and we tried to stop to go in there and couldn't stop. Just slid right off the line. So we went to the bottom of the hill, got turned around. We must have made five trips before we got so we could get up

Robert Louis Campbell, 1955, and Mary Martha Albert, 1956

there and get in the yard. We got in the yard and we were the only ones there. I think they had 180 rows of rooms, camps, whatever they are. We went in. It was really snowing, wicked hard. Cars were starting to come in, so I said to her, I'm going over to the vending machine to get what I can get to eat.

I went over there and got some of that peanut butter and crackers and peanuts—a bunch of them—and brought them over.

MARY: We had to live on love that night, I'll tell you.

BOB: Well, everything closed down an hour after we got in there. All the restaurants were closed, the bus lines were down, taxi service was down. Everything closed. We had six bags of potatoes in the car to take to the relatives in Connecticut. Had to lug those in. I went back to get some more peanuts and they were all gone.

MARY: The thing I'll never forget is, we stayed at his mother's that first night. She kept coming in and asking us if we needed anything. It was just her way of being helpful. Bob's folks were the age we are now when we got married.

Then right after we were first married, Bob's mother wrote a letter to us, or to me. Robert and probably Roland [Bob's brother] read it, but Robert never let me read it. I think he destroyed it. They were so Irish and I was a French girl. His mother was very, very stern. I ended up to be her favorite after a while. I used to call my kids little half-breeds because they were half French and half Irish, and that used to get her goat, too.

They had a big wedding reception for us after we got down to Connecticut.

Sis and Sam [Bob's sister and her husband] had met each other before, and he called her and invited her someplace. We had the trailer and he drove in the driveway. Roland and Evie's [Bob's brother and his wife] house was up the little hill where Sis lived. Sam was about ready to knock. The dog barked, and I opened the door and hollered, Shut up! And it was Sam standing there. He was looking for Sis.

I didn't know anybody except Roland, Evie, and Sis. Bob's brother liked to tease, especially with French jokes. I made up my mind I wasn't going to let it bother me, so I just ignored him. He quit after a while.

After we got our trailer, we went shopping for groceries the first time at Mertz Department Store. We bought all kinds of stuff—silverware, spices, and all the little incidentals. It came to $288. We had the money but we didn't think it was going to be that much. I still have a couple forks left from that. I was homesick, but after a while, my sister Toni, Mom, and Dad came down. I have pictures of you all in the trailer. Remember that Kennedy kid? You girls had a crush on him.

The first fall we were down there, Robert brought Sharon and me home for harvest, and I picked potatoes at Campbell's. Mrs. Campbell took care of Sharon. I picked potatoes for Freeland Smith that fall, too. We came home for good the following spring.

I don't remember being lonesome in Connecticut, but it was an adventure, especially getting there. We lived there for a year and a half.

BOB: Too long! Worked on a dairy farm.

MARY: I was pregnant with Sharon. She was the only one born in Connecticut. That was his weekend to do the chores on the farm and he had me helping him. He wanted me to move the pickup ahead. They had a hayrack. It was in reverse, of course, and I backed into him and pinned him between the tailgate of the pickup and the hayrack. He kept telling me to put it in gear and go ahead, but I didn't. We pushed it. He ended up in the hospital. The next day I went into the hospital to have Sharon and he came in with me. He was on crutches, so they brought the wheelchair for him!

l–r: Leo and Azilda Guerrette, Mary, Bob, Lizzie and John Campbell,
February 6, 1956

BOB: The dairy farm job in Litchfield, Connecticut, was a perfect job. I worked for a millionaire, Joseph D'Assern, a stockbroker on Wall Street. She was a Walker. Her family owned a New York steamship line. It was a hobby farm with 17 head of cattle, 50 hens, and every once in a while, he'd have some sheep. He'd have parties in the summer. We'd get everything ready for his visit in the summer. We lived in a house trailer. They had a nice house. They had three or four maids there all the time. They used us awful good there. They had a Maine Day. They brought in the lobsters, Maine potatoes, and champagne. When they brought the champagne and dropped it off at our house trailer, I had to sign for it, and it was $1,700. For one party! Anything you wanted was right there all the time. There was hot butter there, and it wouldn't even start to get cold, and they'd take the butter away and put you another one down.

23

Loretta, Mary, Bob, Peter

MARY: Your champagne glass never got empty. My sister-in-law Evelyn kept dumping her champagne in the flowers. When you're not used to drinking that stuff in the middle of the day, you know. I told her she was going to kill the flowers and she did.

BOB: Mrs. D'Assern's brother had Ferraris and all these fancy race cars. My brother worked there, too. That's how I got in there. We didn't know a damned thing about those cars. We were two hicks and we didn't know how to move them things around.

They were away and we were cleaning out the barn and our coveralls were dirty. We'd never seen an automatic washing machine before, top loader, never used one. Went up, thought we'd throw the

clothes in that, then we'd go to town, come back, they'd be all
washed and we'd put them in the dryer. They had this great big box of
Tide sitting on the floor, so we looked in there and it said SOAP and it
also said AUTOMATIC WASHING MACHINE, so we thought we'd help the
maids. We picked that box up and filled that washing machine full of
soap, turned it on, and went to town. We come back and stopped in
to see how it was doing. We had a hard time getting the door open.
Soapsuds about three feet high in there. That machine was just going,
whooh whooh. Stuff coming out, just like shaving foam. The entryway
was as as big as these two rooms, with a step-up six or seven inches
high into a great big kitchen, and soapsuds were going out into the
kitchen. There was a trapdoor going to the cellar. We opened up the
trapdoor, went to the barn to get a squeegee, and we pushed and
hosed it all over the lawn. The cellar way was full of soap but we got it
all cleaned up before they got home. We found out that an automatic
washing machine didn't take soap automatically.

They were awful nice people. They used us real good. But we
hated Connecticut. You get up in the morning, couldn't even put your

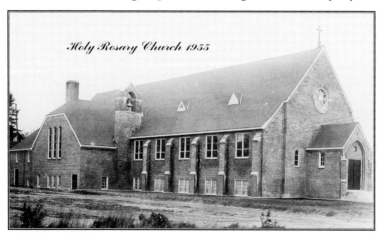

*Holy Rosary Church, 1955
Caribou, Maine*

25

clothes on. Try to take a shower—couldn't. Too hot! Too humid! And you still couldn't get your clothes on. Couldn't sleep at night, stay up at night with your head out the window. No, didn't like it at all. If you did anything for anybody, they wanted to pay you. If they did something for you, they expected to be paid. That wasn't a way of life at all. I didn't care for that at all.

MARY: It was hard to make friends out in the country, and I didn't drive.

BOB: We moved from Connecticut back to Dad's farm in Caribou on the East Presque Isle Road. My folks were from Caribou. Dad come over from Lakeville, New Brunswick, Canada. His second farm was in Caribou on the Presque Isle line near McGlinns', the home of William and Ida Campbell and my cousins, Wilma, John, Peter, Cecelia Mary, Herbert, Charlie, and Tommy. My father died there.

When we got the trailer home to Maine, we got it set up and lived in it for a while. Damned thing, it was so cold, your clothes would freeze right to the wall. We had a real cold, cold winter, so Mom and Dad insisted we stay in the house with them because we

Campbell farm on the East Presque Isle Road
Caribou, Maine

had the kids down there. We already had four or five kids living with us in the trailer, slept in bunk beds in two rooms.

MARY: It wasn't easy living with his folks, but you know, I'm the kind of person, I think, that can get along with mostly anybody.

BOB: But it was difficult at times.

We used to have a store and a filling station out by the road. We moved the store down back and built onto it and that's what we made for a picker shack [a small house located in the back of the farm property for a migrant crew from Canada or the Allagash to live in while they helped with the potato harvest]. The store sat up on cedar pillars for two or three years. Then we went down and started fixing it up to live in. We made it over into our house, so we called our house the little house. It was 16 feet by 16 feet and 24 feet by 24 feet.

So we put the trailer up beside the road to sell. It set there for three months, four months and nobody ever come in. We thought we'd have to haul it to the dump. All of a sudden this guy come in. In his slow drawl, he asked what we wanted for it. I told him $3,800. Said he'd think it over. He came back in a week. Would you take $3,500 in cash? He gave us the $3,500 and came to get the trailer. I knew he had his own house, so I asked him what he was going to do with the trailer. I gotta get something for the wife, Carol. The damnedest thing happened. I work away [in the

Receipt from the filling station

woods] all week. Came home on the weekend, cleaned up and got into bed, and she told me she was filing for divorce, that she was seeing someone else. . . . The trailer: it's her settlement on the divorce.

That's how I got rid of my trailer. It's a good thing they had a fight.

I farmed for a total of 18 years. We raised Katahdin, Superior, and Cherokee varieties of potatoes. There are so many more varieties nowadays. The first year I farmed on the Strickland Road, I hired a crew from up to St. Francis—the Walker family. They lived on the East Presque Isle Road. Pretty near every night I'd get a call. There'd be a fight going on and I'd have to go over and straighten it out. Somebody teased the cook or didn't like her cooking, or somebody was sleeping with somebody's woman or something. There was always something going on. I'd go over and I'd spend about 20 minutes and everything'd be all fine and away we'd go again. It was getting along, pretty near the last of digging. This jobber I had, he had a brother that come down with an old pulp truck. Well. He was going to pick potatoes and be a section foreman. I always hired some trucks to haul potatoes to Caribou. He wanted to put his truck on hire to go. Well, the thing was about a foot and a half higher than the rest of the trucks we had. He had no barrel loader and he had no stake pockets so he could tie the barrels on. No, we didn't want that at all. That made him mad. The barrels were never in the right place and that made him mad. He kept crabbing all the time. My father was about 70 years old at the time and he was doing the digging with the Massey tractor that I bought from Roy Belanger. He went on down through digging and this Bob Walker guy was just raving and ranting. And he took his shirt off and he threw that on the ground and he was all bare and ready to fight about all this. Well, the old man, he always wore a frock and a sweater or a vest under it. He stepped up on the seat of the tractor, stepped over on the tire and he

Original Campbell farmhouse, circa 1932, Caribou, Maine

Little house and Campbell farmhouse as it looks today, Caribou, Maine

jumped off and jumped right on that guy's shirt, and he just trampled that right down in the ground. Then he looked up and he said, Oh, shit! Too bad—I thought you was in it!

That guy never said another word to him. Dad was a great one. Here he was, an old man, and he jumped on that shirt.

It wasn't easy times. Second year of farming I had my back go on me. It was right during digging time. I stayed at the Caribou

29

Thirteen *is* a Lucky Number

Hospital for 10 days, went to Portland, got operated on there. Two years later I had my back go again. Went to Bangor, had it done up there. At first, when I'd gone pretty near two years with my back gone, they kept telling me it was in my head, even when I went to Portland I had myelograms. I had a disc gone in my back. Back then, they had a needle about the size of the leg on a chair. They used to take the blood out of me and then they'd put dye in, take the dye out and put the blood back in. And they'd turn me upside down. Oh, it was painful. Headaches. Oh, my Jesus, they were unreal. I had three or four of them, and it never showed up that I had a disc ruptured. So, I went to Portland to a Dr. Maltby and he put me down on the table, turned my ankle, and I came off that table about ready to kill him. Well, he says, I'm quite sure I know what the problem is. The only thing is, you've got to give me consent to go in and operate and you're going to be asleep when I do it, and you'll have to trust my judgment—what I do.

I told him he could take a jackknife and cut that leg right off there without even putting me to sleep if he wanted to because that leg just drove me crazy.

I can fix that. Come back in a week, he said.

I had no place to stay when I got down there, so I went and stayed with on old Irish relative in South Portland for about a week. She played the accordion and sang to me. I wanted to sleep on the floor. All she had was feather ticks for me to sleep on, and I had to sleep on them because she wouldn't let me sleep on her floor. So, I got hold of my cousin, Cecelia Mary Campbell. She came and got me, and I went to her place and had a sleep. She had more remedies for me.

MARY: In 1969 we moved up to the Ashby farm. We rented up there on the ridge. We lived in Presque Isle, had a Caribou address, and a Fort Fairfield phone number. We were there eight years.

Bob: We had barn dances at the Ashby farm. This is how we got them going. We used to go dancing up to Pete's Maple Grove on Long Lake and we went over to the dances at the NCO Club at Loring Air Force Base, so we decided we'd have some stuff going on down home. We bought a couple of big hams and had a feed. We'd set plywood on barrels for tables and have old benches to sit on. Called around the neighborhood to see who'd bring stuff. Then we had a place to put the drinks, so to have it all in one place. Anybody could drink what they wanted—whatever. Everybody shared and shared alike.

So we had dinner and we had mostly record players for the dance. Then we asked The Fabulous Fables from the NCO Club to come over and play. They started playing at nine o'clock at the base. We started at 3:30 or 4:00, so we'd have them come over and eat. We'd feed them if they'd play. Well, they came in and played. Gee, it came quarter to nine, they were still there having a good time. One of the guys said, We gotta go!

After the barn dance, l–r, Kim, Janet, Joan

They called them up over to the base and told them they were going to be a little late, and they left. Mary had to take some of them over.

We used to have some great times there at our dances. Good feeds. Mary'd make a great big pot of beans and we'd have two hams. Other people would make rolls and potato salads, green salads, whatever. They came from all over the place. We used to have up around 300 there. It was a great big barn, 60 feet wide and 100 feet long. We stored potatoes in there in the winter. It was sectioned off—like half of one end was potato house, the other half was shop, and stables. We had cows, hens, pigs, a horse. Then, there was a place to park trucks in the front. It would store 7,000 barrels of potatoes. The only barn that was any bigger was the Howard Nichols barn, even bigger than the Christie barn. The Ashby farm had a big rock on the front lawn that had ASHBY FARMS, written on it. It was quite a novelty because way back in the '50s he paid $3,000 or $4,000 to have that brought in and set there. It has engraved on it a log

Potato blossoms

Is that Sharon driving?

cabin—the same as it was originally farmed. The Ashby farm has never been sold. It was set up to stay in the family. Peter Underwood owns it now. He's the grandson. When the old man died he left it so it would always be in the Ashby family.

Roger and Dave were farming with me. Mom was senile and she always wanted Roland to come home, so he came home and farmed with me. It just got so it was too expensive, and I took a job at the college nights because we only had so many tractors. I had enough family there to run the tractors, so I'd be home in the daytime to tell them what I wanted done. And the government stepped in so strong on farming. I was going to have to buy a new potato harvester. The barn had burned out there at the Ashby farm, so I lost a lot of potato storage and all my equipment. I was going to have to build new potato storage and that was big money. FHA [Farmers Home Administration] said, How do you ever expect to pay it off with a family that size? It's just impossible. You can't do it.

Champion Harvester

So, no loans. I could never get a loan through a bank much, so I worked my way up through different ways. I had some people, Francis Reardon from Boston and big into the New York Stock Exchange, and Lionel Theriault, who backed me. That's how I got financed.

I started in farming in 1961. Mary and I were married in 1956. In 1958 I rented from Stacey Griffin and planted five acres. He'd give me the worst piece of ground he had every year, and I'd get it cleaned up and then he wouldn't rent me the same piece. He'd want me to take another piece. So the bank here in Fort Fairfield, Frontier Trust, had folded, and Northern National Bank took it over. But they had a lot of farms on hand. Ray Johnson was president of the bank. So, he called Dad up and asked if I was interested in taking over a farm in Fort Fairfield. I was 22 years old and I went down to see him. He said, I understand that you're quite a worker and you're wanting to get into farming. We've got a farm Bud Haley and Jack Sprague ran for us and they put peas on it. The hail hit it and they just walked away from it. If you take and plow it under and pick the rocks off it, you can farm it for one year for nothing if the price of potatoes isn't good. If the price is good, I'd like to get $10 an acre or whatever for it.

So I said, Okay, I'll take it, and I rented the Giberson Farm. I went into town. I was delivering milk there at the time for Guimond Farms, peddling in Caribou. I went into Lionel Theriault's house, delivering to him. I told Lionel what I had and I asked him if there was any chance how I could get farming. He said, Well, I don't know. I think you can.

He was selling fertilizer at the time. I asked him, Is there a contract we can get or something I can get? Sell enough potatoes to go on that? Lionel said, We'll talk to Francis Reardon and go from there.

Got that. That went through. Got some seed potatoes. We used to get seconds and picked them all over. We did all right doing that. Then I went to Roy Belanger and told him my story, that Francis and

Working the harvester

Dave working the harvester

Lionel were going to back me. I needed some equipment. He set me up with a new tractor and plow. I went to work from there and I planted 72 acres of potatoes, which was a lot of potatoes at that time. We went up to 175. I had 125. Roger planted 10. Roland planted 40. I furnished all the equipment and it just got too expensive. My stuff was wearing out. I paid something like $8,000 for my harvester. Seven or eight years later they were up 30-some-odd thousand. Potato storage was $100,000. So all this I was doing in eight to ten years was hauling the equipment over the rock pile. I thought it was time to quit. I called Carroll Kelley one day and asked him what the price of potatoes was. He told me and I said, Okay, I got 1,200 barrels of potatoes. I'd like to haul into you.

He said, Okay.

I hauled the potatoes to him and went to see Mary at the Viking Sewing Center, which we owned in Caribou. Mary said, What are you doing in town?

I said, Hauling the rest of our potatoes.

I just quit farming. I called Theriault's and told them I wasn't going to be taking my fertilizer and I quit right then. One day. We got cash and paid all our bills. We didn't owe any.

MARY: We moved to Fort Fairfield on July 4, 1977.

BOB: We moved here all in a day. We filled trucks. They were Arnold Haines's, Roland's, Terry's, and Nason McGlinn's.

MARY: You should ask our neighbors about when we moved here. We had our big farm trucks and the tractors here. I think they thought they were being invaded by aliens—all these kids running around. Fort Hill was *the* street in Fort Fairfield at the time. But they were happy we moved here after a while. When we moved here to Fort Fairfield, I had been in the sewing machine business for two years and Robert got out of farming after that. I cried and cried and cried. I loved farming.

49 Fort Hill Street, Fort Fairfield, Maine

Thirteen *is* a Lucky Number

Bob: We bought this place in about five days and moved in. I was working at the college [University of Maine Presque Isle] washing toilets and scrubbing floors. I told Herb Nightingale that I quit farming. He asked me when I quit. I said, Yesterday!

We had to move off the farm. We had all 13 kids by then, so I had to find a big house. We looked in Presque Isle and Caribou. Nightingale told me there were houses on Fort Hill. We bought the house next door but there was a catch to it. We got a call the next day telling us that papers had already been signed on it the afternoon before. So we called Bernie Gagnon, the owner of the house, and looked at this one. He said, Okay, $40,000. There were two apartments and they were full.

Christ, I didn't even have enough money to buy gas to get down there, so went into Federal Savings & Loan, and Hollis Irving [the bank manager] was there.

Hollis says, Well, Bob, I don't see how you're going to be able to buy a house, with all them kids and everything.

Bernie was there and he said, What the hell does that have to do with how many kids you've got?

Hollis said, But he's got to pay this loan back.

Bernie said, Does he owe you anything? No, well he probably won't owe you anything. I'll take a second a mortgage.

But, I've got to take this before the board, Hollis said.

Well, Jesus Christ. A bank! He came in to borrow money. We ain't going all around downtown and around. Either he's going to get the money or he's not going to get the money. Say right now, are you going to lend it or not? Bernie says, I'm not fooling around. We're in here. We're not just going to dance around with you. We're in to get some money. These people need the house. I want to sell them the house. That's it!

Hollis said, Okay. So he backed us. He gave us a break but he was a hard fellow to get along with after that. This turned out to be a better house. We've lived here since 1977. The first day we were here, Kim went down over the hill on a bicycle and ran into the telephone pole.

We brought all that equipment here to this yard, fixed it up, painted and sold all of it.

The Chandelier

BOB: I made a trip to Mexico. I bought that chandelier out there in the dining room.

MARY: He spent every cent he had.

BOB: Borrowed a little.

MARY: Just went for ride with our son-in-law Terry. He made a trip to McAllen, Texas, to deliver some McCain's products. It was right on the border, so they went to Mexico to eat dinner.

Catholic Church at dusk, Caribou, Maine, 1999

BOB: I went downtown and walked into one place that had all kinds of lights. Looked them lights over. I told her that I liked that light. How much do you want for it?

Something like 9,000 pesos.

For that light?

Yes.

We went to dinner and when we came back by the door she says, Come in, come in, come in. What'll you give me for that light?

I don't know, what's it worth? So we digger-daggered around there for quite a while and figured out what pesos was to America and back and forth.

Oh, no, no, no.

So we left and Terry bought himself some snake boots. We shopped around and when we came back, she was standing there at the door.

Come on in, she says, come on in. So we bought it for $300 and then we had to hire a taxi to have them put it in the trunk and come back across the border. They wanted to know if we had anything.

No, we were just over there for supper. We took it out and then we couldn't get it into the truck cab. The body was all locked up with juice concentrate. We had to take it all apart. It's 100 percent brass. It probably weighs 65 or 70 pounds. It's heavy.

MARY: He came home and he said, You wouldn't believe what I bought. I'm broke!

The next day, he won the Tri-State Megabucks, October 26, 1987. Winning number was: 3-9-12-14-23-33. We bought our ticket at Hendrich's Market.

There were two winners. We won $500,000 and a lady from Vermont won $500,000. We always wanted to meet her.

BOB: It helped us a lot. It's not the big answer, but it certainly helped.

MARY: When we went down to pick up our first Megabucks check, I said, God, when we used to farm we had a lot bigger checks than that! By the time they take the taxes out of the lottery check and all.

Mary Gets Struck by Lightning

MARY: It was in August. A nice hot sunny day. You could hear the thundering off in the distance. And see lightning. Robert was off mowing. I was in the basement of the little house doing laundry and had the old spin-dry washer. I was trying to hurry up, and I had both hands in water and, all of a sudden, the lightning came right through the pipes, hit me. Caught me. I went clear back against the wall in the cellar—24 feet. It picked me right up. I screamed and screamed. Robert's father was in the garden working and he heard me screaming, of course. He came down, and I couldn't stop, so he went out and got Robert and said, Something's wrong with Mary. She's gone crazy or something.

I went in to the doctor and he told me that I would not sleep for a while. And I didn't. I don't know where it hit first, but it ended up with me. It numbed me. For years and years I didn't sleep. Just couldn't sleep. I think it's a woman thing, too. After a certain age you wake up in the middle of the night. I'm getting so now I can sleep pretty good.

Everything else got burned along the way. I was worried about the baby. I was six or seven months pregnant with Joan. She sleeps real well!

BOB: The lightning came in and hit the potato house and blew the chimney right completely apart. I had my trucks parked a few hundred feet away from the potato house, and the bricks hit the trucks. It burnt the wires at every staple. It followed through into the barn, burnt the electrical box and all the lightbulbs. It went from there down to our little house and burnt every lightbulb there, but it didn't burn the refrigerator.

Mary, The Shy One

MARY: I was very shy but what took me away from my shyness was Amway, believe it or not. We used to go to these weekends away and they made you get up in front of thousands of people and talk.

BOB: I said, We can get along without you. I'm going to send you to Europe. She said she wouldn't go. Kim was four years old.

You're going to go. So, I bought her a ticket. She knew but she still said she wasn't going to go. I had Dale Cox take us down to Boston and put her on the plane. She wouldn't even look back at us. That was quite an experience. We didn't know Boston from Chicago. We were looking for a hotel. We drove around, found a vacancy. Got a room. We're there for a while. Pretty near asleep and from the next room, OH HONEY HONEY OH MY GOD OH OH! About an hour later, BANG BANG. Some car backfired.

Got up in the morning, washed up and everything and went outside.

Dale stayed at a friend's house and picked us up. We got on the elevator to go down. Two other guys got on. They said, Did you stay here last night?

Yes, I said.

Did you hear anything?

Not much, heard a backfire or something out there.

You never got hurt or anything?

Well, there was shooting there.

42

Well, we were down in the red-light district. There had been a robbery. People lost their luggage. That backfiring we heard was gunshots, I guess.

CHAPTER FOUR

Family Life

It is something that amazes me today. If we had had seat belt laws like they have today, we would have to have had three vehicles to go anywhere.
~Mary

MARY: People ask all the time why we had 13 children. Bob wanted 17 children. I wanted two. People would ask, How do you do it?

They came one at a time and you loved the next one just as much as you did the others. I wouldn't have done it any different.

BOB: The kids were quite embarrassed about it when they were growing up because different times people would ask them, but then they were glad that they grew up in a big family.

MARY: His parents used to argue all the time. We tried to get the kids to get along. I hated arguing. I couldn't stand it. We never heard our mother and father argue and fight until they got real old at the end. They would argue whether he had taken his medicine or not. One of our daughters was here visiting. She and her husband had a little argument and, of course, the older boy, he came to me and said, Are Mommy and Daddy going to get divorced?

Sharon and Pat having a Kool-Aid and cracker picnic

So they think about that and I'm sure ours did the same thing. Divorce is more plentiful now.

BOB: The best thing I ever did was buy a real good set of boxing gloves. Boy, they used to fight. I mean fight. They'd swing and they'd hit. Neighbor kids would come up here. We had one little feller, Mike Gagnon. He was smaller than the rest. He was kind of frail and he'd stand there and they'd poke him. Once in a while he'd go down and he'd get right back up. You didn't get me yet.

They'd smash him. It was for fun.

After they closed the parochial school [our son] Roger went to the Cunningham School in Presque Isle. They were playing king of the mountain. The others were making fun of the Burke boy and pushing him around. Roger is the same age, but he's a big boy. While Roger went to get help for the Burke boy, the bully pushed the Burke boy off the mountain. Roger went up and pushed the whole bunch off. This one guy was there, and Roger poked his teeth out, and busted his nose. They called Mary to go get him. The principal called that night. He said, I can't blame your boy for what he done. This kid's been causing a lot of trouble. But the way it is here at the school, one has to be treated the same as the other one.

So, he expelled both boys for three days.

That's the thing we always told the kids. If you don't like some-body, say, if you don't like your teacher, remember what she's like. Just when you grow up, don't be like her. But while she's there, you've got to do as she says. And whatever she says, we'll back her. We're not going to back you. You're a kid. We're going to back her. Not just once we said that. We said it quite often—every time they complained.

b: Bob, Pat, Mary, Sharon, Roger
f: Gary, David, Barbara, Mike, Jim

Thirteen *is* a Lucky Number

MARY: Our daughter Kim notices the different ways that her sisters Janet and Joan are bringing up their families. She likes something from both of them. They're both good parents. She said, How can I get both of them into mine?

I told her she'd just have to work at it.

BOB: When Kim asked me how do I do this and that? I said, Well, let me give you the best advice. Any of them damned books you've got. Throw them in the wastebasket. Bring your kid up the way it's supposed to be brought up. Your first instinct is always the best one. You might get beat on it once in a while, but over a lifetime, you're way ahead of the game.

Pat, Roger, Sharon (Barbara in front)

Dave, Gary, Barb, Pat, Sharon holding Mike, Roger

MARY: We used to go for Sunday rides, and the older they got, the more so they didn't like to sit in the car. That is something that amazes me today. If we had had seat belt laws like they have today, we would have to have had three vehicles to go anywhere.

I remember one summer I was going up to Mom and Dad's camp. My sister Loretta, was up there with her kids. Mike and Roger were the same age. Loretta had some kids with her and I had maybe nine kids with me in the car. Of course, those boys were getting big. Coolers and a big tractor tire inner tube on the top of the station wagon. I got pulled over by the cop. He said, Where're you going?

Up to my mother's camp. My sister's up here visiting and I have some of her kids with me.

Well, you're kind of loaded heavy, aren't you?

Yes.

He told me to take it easy. He didn't give me a ticket but I think he was just checking us out. They were fun days up there at the camp.

BOB: When the kids were working, they had to work just like they were professionals. When they got done, they could do whatever they wanted, go play.

My dad was quite a demanding guy, too. He was up into his seventies and he still helped me farm. Then he got a little older, 76 or 77, and not doing so much on the farm, he still had a big garden. He'd say, I want that plowed today!

Well, you might have the tractor on the harvester. We'd have to unhook all the equipment off the harvester and go down and plow that today. Then tomorrow he'd probably want it harrowed, so I'd send a guy down to harrow. Dad says, He don't know what the hell he's doing. You come down and harrow that thing for me.

Did it out of respect for him. Well, everybody. We were planting potatoes when Regina [Mary's sister] got married. We went off to Connecticut to her wedding.

MARY: We had our kids' town friends here all the time. I think it was when Mike was going away to the service, all his buddies came over, and they were sitting behind the house on the lawn singing. Someone called the cops. They thought somebody was breaking into the church. Had to be somebody right around here, I don't know who called. Anyway, the cops came up. They were telling stories and singing. I don't know what they were singing but it was maybe one o'clock in the morning. The whole town knows us, but we don't know them.

There was a young girl who would just come home with Janet. We thought she was Janet's friend. Come 8:30 or 9 o'clock we'd say, You better go home.

No, I don't have to go home.

You can stay here, but you need to call and let your mother know.

Oh, she knows, you don't have to call her.

Joan rides the Viking Sewing Center station wagon in the Potato Blossom Parade in Fort Fairfield, Maine

So, for two or three weeks this girl would come here all the time. A few times I took her downtown. She said they had an apartment down on Main Street, so I'd drop her off. Then, she said something about living with her uncle, and he was going to take care of her.

BOB: Her mother stopped and dropped her off in the yard once, wearing a great big hat. It was the only time we ever saw her, and she was never home. The mother took off with a trucker, so the uncle was looking after the girl.

MARY: We surmised she had nobody to take care of her, and that's why she was coming here. Janet said, Mom, she's not my friend. I don't know, she just comes home with me.

⟫◦⟪

BOB: Pretty near all of the grandkids are scared of me because they know that when I say something, I mean it. They're scared of me, but they respect me. That part I like. I never hugged a kid. It's just not my thing. I like them. I took them everywhere. Just hug and kiss everywhere and playful—that's not for me. I'll shake hands. That's as far as I go. I don't deny anybody for doing it. They can do whatever they want.

CHAPTER FIVE

Trips and Adventures

*When the waitress came to serve Robert his plate, down came
that huge chandelier!*
~Mary

MARY: One trip that I really enjoyed was when all of us girls
went to New York with Mom. That was one of my favorite trips and
nicest trips with my sisters and my mother. It was the first anniversary of Dad's death and she had given us each $500. It was left over
from the funeral expenses and we used it to go to New York City.

We drove to Connecticut, got on the bus to New York and saw
a show, *The Nutcracker*, which included the Rockettes. It was in
December and we went for the day. It was special because we were
all together and the first time in a long time with the four of us.

TONI: After we saw the show we went to this real nice restaurant in New York City called Cattleman's. There were no prices on
the menu and Mom was dying to know the cost of the meal. We told
Mom, We're having a great time spending your money. This is your
money we're spending, what do we care what it costs?

MARY: She wanted to know so bad what the cost of the meal
was. We all paid our own bill. Mine was like $65. And all I had was a
cup of coffee with the meal.

TONI: I think Mom ordered scallops. I said, Oh, Mom, you don't want to know how much it costs. You don't want heartburn, do you?

MARY: Another time when we were all together was when Dad wanted his four Golden Girls to spend the night in Sinclair. It was around Dad's birthday and their anniversary, and we went to spend the weekend. It was so cold—30 degrees below zero. Of course, Mom had short-sheeted our beds and put rice in our beds. We drank a whole bottle of apricot brandy. Mom came upstairs and wanted to know where hers was. It was gone. Then, I think it was Regina who put the empty bottle under Mom's pillow.

Mom gave us a knitting lesson that night. I have never knit. I learned from the nuns when I was going to school but I never kept it up. I hated it. I had always wanted to learn to knit and we thought it would be a good time for her to teach us.

TONI: What else do you do in Sinclair, Maine, when it's 30 below?

MARY: Then, when we went to church in the morning, we gathered all the rice and put it in Mom's purse. We thought when she went for her handkerchief or something in her purse, the rice would come out, but she had wised up. She was smarter than we were. She was a lot of fun.

TONI: After that night we were all in Sinclair with Dad, he was upset the next day when we left, and he ended up in the hospital.

We promised Mom before she died that we four girls would get together once a year.

MARY: When Loretta and Paul (he was in the service) lived out in the country in Rome, New York, we went to visit them. They weren't expecting us and we had a hard time finding them. We drove all around and we were about ready to give up, and finally we found the place. Poor Loretta; they had a party the night before for somebody who was going away, and she was on the couch.

When we had the Viking Sewing Center in Caribou, we had a station wagon and we used to put it in the Potato Blossom Festival parade. The kids would ride on top. One of the advertising things we had were the Viking horns, and they wore them.

We sold the business in 1985 to Dana Allison. Very smart lady. She was one of my really good customers. She came in and would buy $300 or $400 worth of fabric at a time. She made quilts, shirts, and pants for all her boys because they were so tall, they couldn't get anything to fit them.

BOB: Every one of them was smarter than hell. Brilliant and talented. She started out the door one day. She turned around and came back. You're selling this place?

Yes.

I want to buy it.

Just like that.

I'd been to Bangor and had a realtor just three or four days before that. They hadn't even come up or put a sign up. They didn't charge us the full commission.

MARY: In 1975 we took over the Viking Sewing Center after we had backed Gordon Everett, a neighbor, who was already work-ing for Singer. We were getting paid five percent of the sales for our payments. That's how I went to Germany. My sister Loretta was over there and she was very homesick, so a friend of mine, Barb McHugh Buchanan, was supposed to go with me. We got our tickets in February to go in September.

In the meantime, she got a job working at the Presque Isle School Department, so she wasn't able to go. I went myself with a guided tour arranged by Camille Albert at Worldwide Travel. I flew out of Boston and met the group of 49 in London. We visited several countries and came back after Thanksgiving. I didn't know anybody. When I left Madrid to go to Frankfurt, my flight was delayed, and

Thirteen *is* a Lucky Number

Loretta and Paul were waiting for me at the airport in Frankfurt all day long. I was supposed to get there at noontime, and I never got there until night. I had a nice visit with them for two weeks.

I visited another relative, Pat Wooten, on Bob's side of the family while I was there. Loretta took us, and it took us an hour and a half to drive there because of the black ice on narrow, crooked roads. Pat had broken her leg a couple days before and she was on crutches.

I never got mail from home, and they never got any mail from me until just before I got home because they had a mail strike over there in Europe at the time. When I got to Loretta's I had two letters from home waiting for me.

Probably the most memorable part of the trip was when I got home. It was about 72 degrees when I landed in Boston and I stayed overnight. Robert picked me up at the airport. We drove to New

b: Regina, Toni, Loretta, Mary
f: Azilda and Leo Guerrette at their 50th wedding anniversary, 1989

Hampshire and visited family. The next morning, he was shaving or something and the TV was on, and it said they had 36 inches of snow in Caribou, Maine.

Well, Robert said, you must have misunderstood, it must be three to six inches. Call the house and see if the kids are home.

I called. The kids weren't home. They never did make it home the night before. They were everywhere. And, there *were* 36 inches of snow! I had heard right. That was one time when I was right and Robert was wrong.

We went and ate breakfast and then, we couldn't even get out of the driveway because it was all ice. We decided to drive home anyway. We thought if the kids had made it to school, it can't be that bad. You know Aroostook County people—it can't be that bad.

Of all the things to do, we took Route 1, the scenic tour, and it was all snow and snowbanks. The farther north we got, the more snow there was. Some of the roads were closed. The only way we could go was Route 1A to Fort Fairfield. We were living at the Ashby place at the time. We started on the Marshall Road. Couldn't make that because there were cars abandoned on the road.

We had to turn around at Findlen's near Ginn's Pavilion and come back around by Green Ridge. When we got to that sharp corner, we got in the snowdrifts that were unbelievable. Of course, my boots were in the trunk of the car and I had a dress on. We couldn't get through and had to leave our car there and walk almost a mile the rest of the way home. The drifts were something. A little lesson there for dressing properly for the weather.

The plow had to go around our car. The next day Robert got the tractor and dug it out.

That was a long trip home. We got home and there was nobody there! They didn't get home until the next day. It was the blizzard of 1974. The kids stayed at various houses. Some stayed at Perreaults' in

57

Thirteen *is* a Lucky Number

Caribou, some stayed at Griffins'—three different places in Presque Isle—they couldn't all stay at one house. Some of the kids stayed right in the gym at Zippel School.

TONI: We were living on the Caribou-Presque Isle Road and I was working for Mark Kane at Brown's Jewelry Store in Presque Isle. I had taken a cab to work because they were predicting this huge storm. They had taken the kids to school on the buses. Then, I just got to the store, and a bulletin came on the radio that the schools were going to be closing, and the road was closed beyond the Caribou-Presque Isle Bridge. All I could think of was my two children getting home on the bus. I said to Mark, I've got to go.

I took a cab to Zippel School and helped the teacher, Artis Holt. Her husband Thurber and I took all of the kids in his four-wheel-drive to Blotner's Trailer Park before getting to our house. I waded in snow up to my butt and helped them in. The women from Potato Service, and five or six other kids who couldn't get home, stayed at my house.

Then I remembered Mary's kids. I felt so bad that I hadn't thought of them that I called the school and talked to one of them. I think I had 13 staying at my house that night.

<hr />

MARY: Bob used to like to go to Winter Carnival in Quebec City. He had gone with some friends before. One year he decided to take me and we went with two other couples, Amy and Nason McGlinn, and Jeannie and Rudolph Turcotte.

We were in the Marie Antoinette Restaurant eating. Robert didn't come in with us. He was in the car taking a nap. We were almost done eating when he walked in, so he ordered. All the time we were eating, the lights kept flickering. Nason, who worked for

Maine Public Service, kept saying, There's a short in those wires. They're going to have a fire in here.

When the waitress came to serve Robert his plate, down came that huge chandelier! The wire had broken. It had thick glass on the inside and wooden slats all the way around. It hit him over the head. The restaurant managers came and took him to the hospital emergency room. Nason went with them.

When we finally got to the hospital, Amy said, We've got the right place. Robert's here.

We could hear him way down at the end of the hall—talking, telling the doctor he'd never seen such a brain on the X-rays, and all this. He had a big bump on the head and was all black and blue from the bruises on his arms, everywhere. He was lucky he didn't get killed.

After we got home, we got a bill from the hospital, so we called the restaurant. Then we got another bill. After the third bill, we called the Chamber of Commerce in Quebec. We never got another one.

That same trip, I didn't go, but the others went to the Château Frontenac to sightsee and go on the ice slides. When Robert came downstairs, he slipped and fell. When he got down at the bottom of the stairs, he had only one rubber on. He had worn rubbers over his shoes. The maitre d's were all looking for his rubber and didn't find it. When he got back to the hotel, he sat down to take his shoes off, and there's the rubber. He had two on one foot. I'm so glad I didn't go to the Château.

Younger Days

MARY: In my younger days, we used to wear our black (or red) jeans and saddle shoes. Loretta and I used to go roller-skating at Martin's Roller Rink on the Presque Isle Road. We were on the way, so our friends Wes and Wade Smith would stop and pick us up in their panel truck. We were some of the last ones to get in before you get to the roller rink. We'd all pile in the back of that truck. I'm sure everyone in Caribou knows about that. Good old days. I thought I was a good skater and Loretta was very good.

When I met Robert, he didn't like roller-skating, but he told me about the time he went with Chum McHugh and somebody else. They took him around to help him. It was summer and they had the doors open, and they let him go and he skated right out the door. They did it on purpose. That's why he didn't like roller-skating, and he wouldn't go after that.

⫸◈⫷

The funniest time was when I wet my pants up at the Campbells'. I was going out with Robert and we were going to the movies. We stopped at Pete's and he was separating cream. They were telling jokes

Can you find Mary? Mud Lake, 1976

and I got to laughing and I wet my pants. So, Pete thought the separator was leaking. He didn't know if it was oil or water and he actually put his hand in it. It was my most embarrassing moment. The more he tried to find out what it was, the more I laughed. I don't remember what the joke was. Robert told everybody.

Besides babysitting and picking potatoes, my first job was working at Sam's Dairy Bar. I made lobster rolls. Sam and Germaine Albair were such nice people. We worked in the toy store also. I remember counting those little Lionel Train pieces. That's why I never bought them for my kids. We lived right next door. The only thing I didn't like about working at Sam's was walking home at night with the bats in the trees. We were a draw card for the boys. The Washburn guys came around.

TONI: I remember Germaine laughing and saying, Yup, there you go, Mary. He comes here every night for clams or hot dogs just to see you.

Sunday at Mud Lake

61

MARY: I liked the farming best of any of my jobs. It was hard work but I was at home more. I did baking and laundry at night.

The Cottage of Love

MARY: Mom was quite a fisherman.

TONI: The grandchildren have such fond memories of the camp. Mom showed all of them how to fish. The four of us girls wouldn't go fishing with her because she never knew enough to get out of the boat. I'd say, Mom, I have to pee.

Well, she'd say, pee in the water.

TONI: Getting a bite was more important. She took them fishing for barbote [bullhead or catfish] at night or very early in the morning.

MARY: She was nicknamed Madame Barbote. She was brought up on Long Lake and they probably fished a lot. I remember going to

The Guerrette Camp at Mud Lake, near Sinclair, Maine, 1966

Mud Lake from there because the barbout fishing was better. That's how she learned the channels of the thoroughfare.

We were all at Mom and Dad's camp at Mud Lake. Our neighbor Don Holmes had a camp next door. He had this big boat. He liked to go down the thoroughfare that went to Long Lake. He didn't know what the channels were, so he asked Mom to show him the way. A bunch of us, I think there were eight of us, went with him. We left Dad at the camp to watch the kids—all 13 of them.

We went for a ride down the lake and through the channels to Long Lake. We went to Bert's to have a drink and something to eat because it was getting to be suppertime. Don ordered lobsters for all of us, so it was like eight or eight-thirty by the time we left. When we got back to the camp, Dad was mad. He met us at the water. He was so worried about us because it was dark.

The kids were hungry. I guess the older girls Sharon and Pat probably helped cook hot dogs and made peanut butter sandwiches for the rest of the kids. That was really quite an experience because Dad never really got mad. He was a very mild-tempered man, so

Mud Lake, 1974

Mémère at Mud Lake, 1985

when it happened, you really remember it. The only other time I saw him upset was when Toni went through the ceiling.

TONI: When our parents were building the house on Pitt Street, I had gone to play with Linda Bourgoine. Dad had to go down to the hardware store. His last words were, Do not go in the house.

Well, Mary, Loretta, and I went upstairs and started running around on those rafters. That was our ballet-dancing machine. I took a wrong step and I came down through the ceiling. When Dad got home, all the kids in the neighborhood were standing there. He chased me and every time I ran around the house, there was another kid standing there. He was so mad because he was so clumsy and he couldn't run after me. My punishment was to kneel in the corner and I knelt quite a while that day.

Mary, Regina, Loretta, and Toni in front of 1 Pitt Street, Caribou, Maine

Holy Rosary School from Washington St. Early 1960s, Caribou, Maine

Mary and Josephs

TONI: Mary already has the name of Marie [French for Mary] Martha. When Loretta and Paul were getting ready to go to Germany, Loretta needed her original birth certificate to get a passport. They went to St. Agatha, where she had been recorded. Father Soucy, the priest in Sinclair, who had christened the babies, had put Joseph David or—whatever—for all the boys, and Marie—whatever—for all the girls on the baptismal certificates. So, Loretta was Marie Loretta instead of Loretta Marie. She had to go through all this red tape for a passport to be able to leave the country. I don't know if she had any other middle name, but she goes by Loretta Marie.

We were all Marie, all three of the older girls. Regina was okay. When Loretta told me about it, she said, You better go check on your name.

Mom and I went to the town office in St. Agatha and looked at the rest of us. I couldn't believe my eyes. There was a whole list of Maries on the girls' side and a whole list of all Josephs on the boys' side. Instead of changing all my legal papers, I just changed my name from Marie Antoinette to Antoinette Marie. I went to the town office. I don't think I had to pay to have it changed.

Grampie Albert

MARY: When I was young—eight or nine years old—I was at my grandparents'. I went to visit and play with my friend Marlene Chamberlain Findlen. There were no adults around. Three or four of us went swimming in Long Lake across from the Chamberlains' house. There was gravel in the water and it was a nice place to swim,

Marie (Ouellette) and Fred Albert, Mary's grandparents

but when I was walking out, I tripped and fell. It wasn't that deep but I panicked. Marlene pulled me out.

I was late getting back home, so Grampie Albert came looking for me. We were just getting out of the water. He cut a little branch off a tree, gave me one whack, and followed me all the way home. One whack, but it felt like it was all the way home. He was a little guy, but he had a temper. I was punctual after that. After that, if I went to play, that's what I did.

To this day I'm afraid [of water]. I took swimming lessons for three years so I could take a shower without thinking of it and panicking. I'm still not a water person.

Toni, Romeo Ouellette, Mary, Regina, and Loretta

Grampie Albert's name was Alfred, but everybody called him Fred. He had a sawmill and there were logs in the water all the time there. Those logs. We used to go run on those and turn them. They also had a store in their house. The only thing I remember were the candy bars.

TONI: There were stores in a lot of homes. Grammie used to sell bread and whoopie pies. Mom and Dad used to take us up there on Sunday, and they would stand us three older girls on the showcase. Remember how we used to sing? Little songs like, "How Much is that Doggie in the Window?" "You Are my Sunshine."

MARY: Then they would give us a shiny quarter for entertaining people.

I remember the game wardens coming to inspect the property for venison—in the ice house and even down cellar, where Grammie had her canned venison.

Uncle Joe and Aunt Sophie Albert were my godparents.

I used to babysit for Uncle Bill and Aunt Armance Albert and all those kids. I think she had 16. Then I turned around and did the same thing.

Sinclair Adventures

MARY: We three girls were around eight, nine, and ten. We'd go scout the Sinclair neighborhood. Mrs. Dumond had her bread raising

Mary's birthplace in Sinclair, Maine

on her back porch. We went and got the bread and we were throwing it at each other. There was bread everywhere. That poor woman.

When I first got married and started making bread, I thought of Mrs. Dumond all the time.

Mary, Loretta, Azilda, Leo, Toni (Regina in front)

CHAPTER SIX

Sugar Beets

*He [the sheriff] came in with all his guns on, and we were
eating supper. I said, What can I do for you?*
  ~Bob

Bob: How I got started in the sugar beet business was when
Fred Valsing (he was from New Jersey but he had farms in Texas) was
up here, and he brought all kinds of politicians with him. He had
with him Governor Kenneth Curtis and U.S. senators John
Hathaway and Edmund S. Muskie, really pushing for sugar beets.
They threw a great big dinner and I went to it, and I signed up to get
into it.

Then, when I found out you had to get equipment, I grew
more than I should have, probably. But then, I took care of other
people's acreage, and dug their crops. Because the equipment cost so
much, I had to have enough to make it go.

I used to plant around 60 acres of sugar beets myself, in addition to 110 acres of potatoes. I also took care of Red Smith's and
Phil Crandall's sugar beet acreage.

Then, I had the kids work in the sugar beets. That was quite a
job because you had to thin and weed them. The weeds, mustard and
everything, were a big problem. The kids worked at that all summer

long. They picked rocks all spring and pulled weeds all summer. They learned how to work. They got so they knew they didn't want to do that, so they learned to get into something else.

I think it was a thing that could have went, but I'm glad that it didn't. After I got out, the price of sugar dropped. It was no good anymore. If there had been a price for sugar, I'm quite sure we could have grown them. After having sugar beets on it, the ground was so nice to grow a crop of potatoes on. The sugar beet roots went down big and deep, and the ground broke up and was mellow. The next fall when you dug potatoes, the dirt would fall right through the lags of the digger. Then you plowed the sugar beet tops under. It was a very nice rotation crop. I enjoyed it to this extent: You could ruin your crop very easily by making mistakes, so as you planted them and watched them grow (and they grow fast), you could see how good you were doing or how bad you were doing. I took a pride in what I was trying to do, so I was satisfied with it. I know a lot of people who weren't satisfied with it. I'm not saying they did right or wrong, or maybe the ground wasn't just right for it, but for me, I was satisfied with it. I got paid. Some others didn't.

MARY: Robert got paid!

BOB: I have some good stories on that. One of the deals was that I never grew russet potatoes, never did. Valsing, Inc. promised you so much money if you'd grow so many acres of beets and potatoes. So, I did that with them. I would sell the potatoes in the fall and they'd pay us. That would help us pay for the potato farming and fall help. Then, we'd dig the sugar beets. Come to find out, when I went and got my potato checks, Fred Valsing had a mortgage from the sugar factory, Valsing, Inc., so the check was made out to Robert Campbell and Valsing, Inc. After I signed it, and then they signed it, they would take it to pay on my bill for the sugar beets—the seeds and fertilizer to grow the sugar beet acreage. So, I was winding up with nothing. So, I went in and told them I had a big family and needed the money. I'd gone over there quite a few times, wanting my money.

Oh, can't give it to you, they said.

They said after I left the day before, Fred was in. I went in there one day. I had a paper bag with me. I set down on the bench in the office upstairs. They wanted to know if they could help me.

Yuh, I said, I've come to get a check for my sugar beets.

Oh, we can't give it to you. Fred has to give it to you.

I said, That's all right. So, I went and set down.

They said, He's not here.

Oh, that's okay. I'll wait until he comes.

Well, he might not be here this afternoon.

I said, That's all right. I'll set right here.

So, when it come time for them all to go home, they said, We're closing up.

I said, That's all right. I'm all set. I've got food right here. I'll wait until Fred comes.

You can't wait.

Seems as though I've got to. If he always comes in that early, I'll stay here in case he comes in. In the meantime, I need the money.

Oh, no, no, no. He won't be here tonight.

Finally they convinced me to go home.

I told them I'd be back there in the morning. And I was back there in the morning when they opened up. I went in and before noon, I had my check, because I had my bag with me again, and I was staying until Fred come in. I wasn't going out to eat. I was going to eat right there. I didn't talk to him that day.

There were two separate companies. Maine Sugar supplied all the spray material and seed for the sugar beets. Well, you owed for that, so when I got my check for my potatoes, they wanted to apply

73

it to what I owed for sugar beets. But I didn't sign it. I kept it. I wouldn't do that.

They told me there was no way to get around it.

I said, Oh yuh, how much do I owe you?

They told me how much it was. So, I told them I'd make them out my personal check for that, so I wrote the check out to Maine Sugar and Robert Campbell. I filled the check out for the amount and give it to them.

Oh, oh, you can't do that.

I can't?

No.

Why can't I?

Because that's illegal.

That's what Valsing did. They put it right down here. His name is on it. He's going to endorse it. When Fred Valsing comes to see me, I might sign it, after he signs it, but I'm going to wait until then. I've got you all paid, so give me that check and let me cash it on my own because my bill I owe you is paid. As far as you're concerned, it's right there in that check. As soon as I deposit this, it'll be there—what I owe you. The rest of this is mine.

They didn't know what to do about that, but I said, That's all right.

Two or three days later, the sheriff, Luther McLaughlin, come and served papers on me. He came in with all his guns on, and we were eating supper. I said, What can I do for you?

He kind of laughed a little bit and said, Bob, I've got some papers from Maine Sugar. You've got to sign this paper.

Won't do it.

I'm not here to do anything about it. My job is to just serve you the paper.

That's all right. When you go back, you can tell them my check is there, and all they've got to do is do what they got to do. I figure I'm right.

It was about two to three days later, a couple of men come out and talked to me.

Bob, don't be so silly. Don't be so silly. Everybody's signing this. Everybody's doing this. Just do it. It's just the run of the business. We're all right. You'll get your pay.

I know I'll get my pay. But when they make that check out to me, then I'll take mine back and we'll do business the right way. I'm not doing this hiding behind the barrel. I'm coming straight out front. I signed a contract up front to start with you. I want this up front, right now.

So, they paid me in full. I got my pay every time I went in. That was the last year of sugar beets, too. That's when nobody else got paid.

They took on more than they could handle and couldn't keep up. I put my harvester away and people came to me and said, I can't get my beets done. You've got to come and do them.

I said, It's in the contract what I had to do. But I dug a lot of beets afterwards.

The price of sugar went down. Then Valsing couldn't get enough people to grow sugar beets. He lost the whole thing, and he died a poor man. But he did a good thing for the town of Easton. McCain's bought the potato processing plant. J. M. Huber Corporation bought the sugar plant, and they make pressboard.

CHAPTER SEVEN

The Accident

I don't know how to say it. She lost control of the car.
~Bob

BOB: The car accident [on May 15, 1984] really changed our lives a lot. The girl was a very good friend of Joan's. She used to come here to eat.

MARY: She had been here the night before for one of the girls' birthday parties.

BOB: It was a cold, raw day in May around four o'clock in the afternoon. It was thawing and the water was running down the road. A stupid cat ran out in front of her, and she swerved for the cat. The cat turned around and went back. Never crossed the road.

I don't know how to say it. She lost control of the car. We were meeting her. She came over in our lane, went right straight back where there was a steep bank. I thought she was going to go down over the bank. Mary said, Look at her—there she goes!

But she turned back again and came back out of the ditch and across the road again toward us and we hit head-on. Her car spun around and the back of her car went into the back tire of our van. It pushed it hard enough, so it threw it back around in front of us again. It was a most unusual accident.

MARY: We looked and looked and couldn't see the driver. We didn't know where she was. She was pinned underneath and the car was sitting on top of her in the ditch.

BOB: People came and were going to try to lift the car up. Dan Foster's wife came. She was a nurse, and she stayed right there until seven o'clock at night—until the coroner came. And she hung right onto her hand the whole time. The girl was already dead.

The way the officer explained it was, when she hit, she came right out through the passenger-side window. The car came around, hit our back wheel, and when her car came back around, it picked her up and took her with it.

We both had medical problems from it—over $90,000 worth. We were self-employed and with no money coming in, we sold the Viking Sewing Center in Caribou. We had health insurance but it wasn't our fault. They put a binder on the money that we were getting.

They were underinsured on her end. They had $50,000 for coverage and it came to $90,000.

We had $50,000 worth of insurance, too. Our van had insurance. They each paid no-fault insurance.

MARY: They paid 64 percent of his bills and 50 percent of mine because I didn't have as many injuries.

When we got our checks, the lawyer took his money. He didn't charge anywhere near what he could have. Normally, he would get a third. He charged us a quarter. The insurance company took 10 percent off the top for their paperwork. We didn't even get our salary out of it. We were two years out of work and two years recovering. We went behind on our house payments.

BOB: The worst part was the girl's mother. I think, even today, she hates our guts. She blamed us for it.

That's okay. That's fine. Her sister and brother never held it against us. They give us a hug when they see us.

CHAPTER EIGHT

Bob in Dallas

Here I am in a money town. Me with a J.C. Penney 20-year-old jacket on.

~Bob

BOB: We went out to Dallas, Texas, and were going to all the meetings for the sewing machine business. I asked at the hotel where we were staying if they had Rotary Club meetings. He said, Yes, it was just two or three blocks down the street. Just jump on the bus and go right down to it.

The next day I got up, put on my sports jacket and pants, and went down and found the place, right handy where President Kennedy got shot. I went in and, gosh, it was a great big place. I didn't know where it was, so I asked, Do you know where they have the Rotary Club meetings?

Yeah, it's right upstairs.

I walked in and here's all these men dressed up in these great big suits, so I walked over to one of them and says, Is this here the Rotary Club meeting?

Yes, it is, he says. Are you a Rotarian?

I said, Yuh.

He says, Where are you from—here?

I said, No. I'm from Maine.

Oh, my goodness gracious, glad to have you here.

So, I says, Well, what do you do here for the dinner or luncheon?

Go right over and see that woman. She takes the money for everything.

So, I went over and said I was in the Rotary Club and would like to join the meeting. I showed her my card. Oh, she said, you're from Maine. Well, that's great. We have soup and sandwich or you can have the meal.

What's the difference?

It's $7 for the soup and sandwich and it's $20 for the meal.

I'll have the soup and sandwich. I'm not very hungry. She gave me the ticket for soup and sandwich. I talked to some of the guys there. Not too much, got a little conversation in here and there.

I went in and set down at a table, great big round tables. These guys all come in and set down. And, holy gosh, they were dressed like you couldn't believe.

They asked me where I was from. I told them northern Maine. They wanted to know what I did.

I was a potato farmer and used to grow potatoes. Now, I have a grocery store in Easton and we had sewing machines and a mono-gramming business. They were very interested in hearing about all that and they wanted to talk. I asked one of the guys what he did. Executive of an oil company. Another one had an insurance company. Another one was a big accountant somewhere. I was setting with all these great big things in it, and they was putting me at the head of the table, doing all the talking. It was kind of funny.

They always have these fines. That's how they raise their money. Fines are set. They had this guy's birthday, so they all sang "Happy Birthday" to him. Then they had a fine for him and it was $1 for every pound he weighed. He weighed pretty near 200 pounds, but they kicked that over and they laughed. I thought, holy God, that was a big joke.

MARY: Around here it would be just a dollar fine. Period.

BOB: I set there and took that all in. The New York fire chief was coming to Houston, so they said the next meeting was going to be there. The parking would be $15 and the meal would be $150. Everybody was all for it and going to go. Here I am in a money town. Me with a J.C. Penney 20-year-old jacket on. We did a lot of talking and I enjoyed it. I thought, this Rotary is really a network because they say you're welcome into wherever you want to go. I was really welcomed in there, and I was as far out of line as you could possibly be, because some of them were professors at colleges and presidents of colleges. There were 80 or 90 people at the meeting.

When I come out of there, I was waiting for the bus to come up through to go back to the hotel. A feller come over and says, You say you're from Maine?

Yuh.

You're in the sewing machine business?

Yuh. What do you do?

He says, I'm a contractor here in Dallas. By the way, do you have any free time?

I says, I don't know—like what?

Well, come over to supper some night and you can see my shack.

I'll see about that. I'll have to talk to the wife and see. Quite a big contract business?

Pretty good size, he says. Yeah, I started in doing carpenter work for a guy here around 1956. Right next door there was a restaurant that burnt out. The wife and I were going around working my off hours for neighbors fixing up attics and rebuilding things for them. We was trying to get ahead. So, I said to her, Why don't we try to buy that building down there that burnt and fix that up inside. It's right there in the middle of Dallas.

She said, Okay. I went to get a loan and they had an awful time over it because it burnt and I didn't have money behind me. Finally, I convinced them to let me have the money to fix the building. We worked for over a year on that. God, just couldn't sell it right then, so I rented it. Took the rent money and bought another one and fixed it. Kept doing that along and selling some. Then real estate jumped. It didn't matter what you did. You couldn't go wrong. It just grew, and grew, and grew, so I grew with it.

His house is on Main Street, which is a rich section of town. But he had a shack. He invited me down, and he give me a card.

Come on down and we'll have supper and set around the fireplace and enjoy an evening.

But we had a meeting at the hotel for the sewing machines. It was really something to come from nowhere and walk into there and be with high uppie-ups and be welcomed.

I took a Maine banner to give them and they gave me one from Texas.

CHAPTER NINE

The Hill

We heard it coming, but it was foggy. We didn't know where it would land, so we hid in the empty barrels.
       ~Bob

BOB: This is the Parker farm that I farmed for about three years: 1970 to 1973. Lester Parker was a great storyteller. Any time you were with him, he'd have a story. When I was digging and the women were working on the harvester, he liked to be around the women, so he'd get on and tell them stories. One of the stories that Mary's mother liked was when one of the women said, Lester, were you ever married?

Oh, yes, he says, I was married before.

How many wives did you have?

I had three wives.

They said, No.

Oh, yeah. I had three wives.

What happened to them?

When I got married, I bought the farm, and the house had a dirt cellar. The wife went downstairs one day and she seen these mushrooms growing in the cellar floor. So, she cut them and took them upstairs and she ate them. And she died.

Oh, what did she die of?

They were poison mushrooms and she ate them. She died.

Oh, that's too bad. How about your second wife?

Oh, yeah. I was married to her too long before she died.

What did she die of?

Brain concussion.

Brain concussion?

Yes, brain concussion.

What happened to her?

She wouldn't eat the damned poison mushrooms.

We've just gone by where Ginn's Pavilion was. It burned.

This is Andy McGlinn's farm. That's where Andy and Roger farmed. They had the Ashby farm, too. They farmed half and half. Then Roger got done and Andy bought him out. This is barley growing here. There are so many new varieties of grain now.

This is the East Presque Isle Road. If you went to the end, you would come to the bridge. This was Peter Campbell's farm. The Blackstone boys have it now. Pete's son and daughter still live here. This used to be Bill and Ida Campbell's farm. My cousin's daughter lives here now.

Amy McGlinn lives in the last house in Presque Isle. Now we're at the first farm in Caribou. This was my father's place on the left. There's the little house. It used to be the pickers' shack. Before that, the little part of it was a store.

A potato house used to set right here. And there was a great big barn just this side of the little house.

MARY: The house used to be white. Now it's painted yellow.

BOB: You can see the bend in the Aroostook River. The land went clear to the river and three-quarters of a mile up that way. Just past the house is where the kids had a picnic ground and went camp-ing. My father kept it all fixed up nice and trimmed out.

We're going by Haleys'.

We'll go up to the Price hill. Turn here, Mary.

MARY: There's NO TRESPASSING signs.

BOB: I don't give a goddamn, just go. She worries more about the little things.

This is the first farm I owned. Bought that in 1968. I sold it to John Haley. This is where Sharon and them used to drive the fertilizer up over the hill.

We used to come down over this hill on toboggan. There was Tom Campbell, Jim Haley, and myself. We came over this yes, ma'am, diversion ditch. There used to be a tree here. We went right over that tree and busted that toboggan all to pieces.

There was a ski tow from here down. I put the ski tow on a truck and someone took it out of gear and let the truck go. It come down over this hill. The seats went one place and the ski tow went another place. The ski tow was tied to the truck body but it fell off and got banged up.

I used to send an old guy down over with the old tractor with a bulk trailer on it full of potatoes. If it had hand brakes, you'd have to pull them. He went down around there. He must have been doing 40 miles an hour.

Over there is where the tractor and harvester got away with me. I finished the field down there and I dug up here after a rain. I dug all right, but in the shade of the trees, the ground never dried out, and when I turned right, I knew I'd lost it and the tractor wouldn't hold. I told them all to jump off the harvester but it wasn't even going a half-mile an hour. Well, no, they wouldn't jump off. Mary's mother, Aunt Ella, and Pat were on there. We went all the way down. I had an awful time holding that thing. I'd have jumped off, but they didn't jump off.

MARY: We used to have water tanks up there and you'd swear to God you were going to tip over. During the lunar eclipse, we'd come up here and camp out.

BOB: Mary, go right, and go way up on the top of the hill. Now, you're going to have to go! You like coming up here? Keep going, Mary. They can look when they get to the top.

MARY: *Well*, Robert. I *know* the way.

BOB: You can look over and see into Loring. You can see Mars Hill and Presque Isle. If you go beyond the line fence, you can see right into Fort Fairfield.

This part of the farm isn't being used anymore. It is not set up for the equipment that they've got today. If I still had this, there would be no damned fence up there. There is a right of way to these

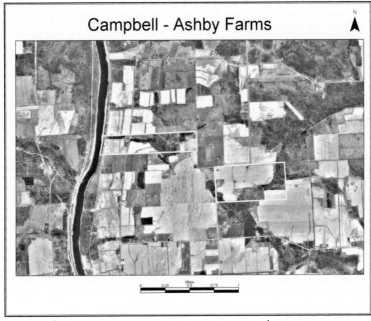

Courtesy of USDA Center, Farm Service Agency, Presque Isle, Maine

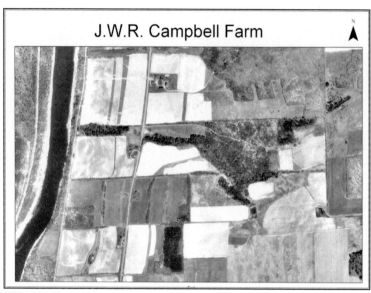

Courtesy of USDA Center, Farm Service Agency, Presque Isle, Maine

farms. Andy McGlinn is farming this now. He's my cousin Nason and Amy's son. Andy plants 300 acres of potatoes and 100 or so of oats.

That was a water tower used for when we sprayed. We pumped water from the brook to the tower. John Haley and Dad had it together. They got their spray water from that.

MARY: One year we had so many potatoes we ran out of storage, so we stored some in that pit. They all rotted.

BOB: This was Dad's farm up here. This road is a mile long. I don't have any heartaches about this. When I get out of something, I move on. That's in the past.

The rock pile is all grown up. We used to snowmobile up here in the winter and have a hot dog roast.

Step on it, Mary. Step on it.

This is the very back end of my father's farm. When I first come back home from Connecticut, Mary and I started planting four or five acres of potatoes. This is what is called the Griffin farm. We're at the line fence between my father's and the Griffins'. The Griffin farm is what you see here now. Different sections are where I used to plant my five acres of potatoes. It was all grown up for quite a few years. We'd have to get it cleaned up. Next time I'd want to rent five acres, he'd make me take another piece of land.

What we're seeing is a good hundred acres altogether. We're at the picnic site. You can see Mount Katahdin on a clear day. Where you see the line fence and the house over there? Bert Robertson was a pilot flying for the Air Force out of Presque Isle base, and this land we're looking at was his father-in-law's farm, Carl Rasmussen. He was going to Germany with the plane. He told them, When I come over, I'm going to wave goodbye and I'm going to take the ears off the horses.

When he waved, he tipped the plane. The load shifted in the plane and it tipped right up and he couldn't bring it back. The wing went down and come into the ground just in back of that taller tree

View from Campbell Hill, site of two plane crashes

on the line fence and it dug an enormous hole there. You could have
put one big cellar in there.

He wasn't supposed to be going so low but his wife and his
father-in-law were living here and he was just saying goodbye. I think
there were eight people working in the field, picking rocks. He killed
two women. There was a Winters boy driving the wagon. The women
were beheaded and one was cut off at the waist. They laid there.

There were four horses out there. It cut them right in two. He
took more than the ears. He took their guts and everything right out.
The young Winters boy got caught in the propeller and was strewed
out all over that fence. His father would have been all right but he
was coming back with an empty wagon that they hauled the rocks on,
and he run to get his boy off the wagon because the boy was driving
the wagon where the people were picking the rocks. He run to get
him and he got killed, too. I think there were seven on the plane.
Everybody perished. There was one guy that lived and that was Freme
Hitchcock. He and Al Winters went to unload the other wagon that

Three Services Held In Caribou For Local Plane-Crash Victims

Two Caribou Women Among Nine Dead When Medium Bomber Hits Field Crew In Green Ridge Farm Tragedy.

Services were held here early this week for Lieut. Bertrand Robertson, 29, of Greenville Junction, and Eloise Newton, 19, and Ann Theriault, 25, both of Caribou, victims of the bomber crash at Carl Rasmussen farm on Saturday morning that took a total of nine lives.

Four civilians and five air corpsmen were killed instantly when the medium bomber, on a routine flight from Presque Isle, crashed into a rock-hauling crew, of which the two women were members.

Two horses were also killed in the crash, which is still under investigation by officials at the Presque Isle Army Air Field.

The accident occurred less than one-half mile from the spot of a bomber wreck last September. The farm is in the Green Ridge section near the town line, five miles from town.

Lieutenant Robinson was the son-in-law of Mr. Rasmussen, the owner of the farm.

Other civilians killed were Alfred Winters, 38, of Presque Isle, a Rasmussen employee, and his son, Alfred, Junior, 9.

Army personnel killed, in addition to Lieutenant Robertson, were Second Lieut. Herbert Myers of Portland, First Lieut. Edward Hankinton of Morrice, Michigan, S/Sgt. William Jochim of Louisville, Nebraska, and T/Sgt. John Keeser of New York City.

The services for Miss Theriault were held at the Holy Rosary Church on Monday morning. Pall bearers were her brothers-in-law, Herbert Cote of Connecticut; Felix Cote of Hartford; Berton Brayall of Fort Fairfield; and Roy McClusky of Grand Falls.

Started Work Last Fall

Miss Theriault, the daughter of Mr. and Mrs. Soloman Theriault,

was coming back. Mr. Hitchcock got some shrapnel in the back. He never was up to health after that, but he was a good man.

I was a kid then, five or six. I was born in '37 and I think this happened in July of '43. We were picking rocks in front of the barn at Mom and Dad's place, and you could look right up on the hill and was born in Drummond, New Brunswick, and spent a good part of her life at Green Ridge, where she received her education in the public schools.

Her father had worked on the Rasmussen farm for nine years and his daughter started working there last fall. She is believed to have been killed by flying fragments from the big bomber.

She is survived by her parents, and six sisters, Mrs. Roy McCluskey, Mrs. Herbert Cote, Mrs. Freeman Hitchcock, Mrs. Berton Brayall, Mrs. Felix Cote, and Mrs. Romeo Thibodeau.

Services For Miss Newton

Services were held later in the morning for Miss Newton, daughter of Mr. and Mrs. Lewis Newton of Washburn Street, at the Gray Memorial Methodist Church.

Miss Newton was born in Caribou and received her education in the public schools here.

Pall-bearers were Israel Lovely, Norman Beaupre, Wilfred Bishop, Irvine Cameron, Thomas Pye, and Caryl Devoe.

She is survived by her parents, one sister, Mrs. Israel Lovely; three uncles, Tom Howard; Charles V. Howard of Baltimore, Maryland; and Frank Newton of Bradford, Rhode Island; and one aunt, Miss Sadie L. Howard of Presque Isle.

Opposite and this page: Article from The Aroostook Republican, July 1, 1943, with some details about the crash and victims.

Interment was at the Webster cemetery in Limestone at the family lot.

Pilot Native of Sherman

Lieutenant Robertson, who was buried on Tuesday afternoon, was born in Sherman Mills in 1916 and was educated in Aroostook County schools.

He was a former State Policeman, and later conducted a dance orchestra in the county.

He began flying in Caribou in 1939, later taking CAA training at Colby and advanced training at East Boston. He spent three months at Chatham, New Brunswick. He was later commissioned as a first lieutenant in the Ferry Command, and piloted planes to South America, England, Scotland, Africa, Persia, and India.

He is survived by his wife, Hazel Rasmussen Robertson; his parents, Mr. and Mrs. Neill Robertson of Greenville Junction; two sisters, Erma and Roberta, four brothers, Walter and Glenn of Concord and Nashua, New Hampshire, and Paul and Dauglas of Greenville Junction; a grandmother, Mrs. Edwina Daggett of Greenville Junction; and a grandfather, George Robertson, of Smyrna Mills.

The plane is said to have dipped low as it came over the field where the civilians were at work, and suddenly side-slipped, plunged downward and striking one wing on the ground. It then appeared to cartwheel and smashed into the midst of the farm crew, which, with the exception of Freeman Hitchcock of Fort Fairfield, was unable to escape flying fragments.

see all this happen from down there. We heard it coming, but it was foggy. We didn't know where it would land, so we hid in the empty barrels.

Thirteen *is* a Lucky Number

I know we come up here. It happened so fast. It was something.
I was sick. Threw up afterwards because the horses' guts were all out
there.

The Air Force people came over from the base and they quaran-
tined the place for pretty near a month. Dad used to have to get permission to go out and spray or to hoe, and they sent a guy out with
him with a gun to make sure no one picked up anything. They came
in with bulldozers and cleaned it up, filled it back in, and they
farmed over it. I'm sure today they can still bring up pieces of that
airplane, pulleys, gears, anything metal that blew clear up here. If
you had a crop here and you're digging, you'll have some of that
plane come up. You know it's from an airplane because it's nothing
from any piece of equipment. The material's even different.

See the other clump of woods about a mile over there? There
was another plane crash about two years later, and nobody survived
that crash either. That blew up in the air and it come down. It was just
like in the old movies when, if you were born back in the '30s or
'40s, you'd see the planes when they come down, they'd have all this
tinsel and stuff flying out of it and it had that roar—*rrrrrrr*. That's the
way that plane come down and went in that woods. It was an Air
Force plane. I think there were five on it. One guy had parachuted
out, but he was too close to the ground and the parachute hadn't
opened good enough. His head caught in one of the trees and stayed
right there. His head was up in the trees. It's a historical site here.

We like it because we'd come up and you could look for miles
and miles and miles. When you're looking over that way, you're
looking at a good 50 or 60 miles. It's all hilly. Nice. It has so much
color to it. You've got your roads; you've got your grain; you've got
your potatoes, your peas. Broccoli has taken the place of peas and
that's a beautiful color. It's actually a beautiful picture, all painted for
you. So, I like it.

I've been overseas. I've been to Texas. I've been to Florida and Idaho. Why the hell did we waste our time going to them places when you can stay right here and enjoy it all. It's all so much better right here. That's my theory on it.

The leaves are starting to turn.

MARY: This is going to make me cry. Going down memory lane.

BOB: We're back in Presque Isle. This is the Ashby farm as far back as you can see. It goes all the way back to Dad's farm. Nice farm. Nice farm. That was a big barn. The garage is gone, but this was the manure shed. He had rails that went to the barn. He had a cart. He threw the shit in the cart, took it out there, and pulled it to the shed. This farm will never be sold as long as it's in the family. Here's the pond we used to swim in.

I think outside of Andy McGlinn and the Staples family, there's no other farmer who lives along these roads. The land has been bought up and the owners live somewhere else.

CHAPTER TEN

9/11

*It was like I was just glued to the bed. Couldn't move. So, I
tried to call her. Couldn't talk. I could just mumble a little bit.*
~Bob

BOB: I had surgery on my eye between twelve and one o'clock
that day. We went back to the hotel and went out to eat around 7:30
or 8:00. We went back to the hotel. I was sleepy, so I laid down and
went to sleep.

About 12 o'clock I had to go to the bathroom. Well, I started
to get up out of bed and I had an awful time getting up. I got over
and started into the bathroom and, gosh, I couldn't keep my leg
under me, so I jumped over and grabbed the TV, and started to upset
the TV and the bureau all together. I got that straightened out and
got myself into the bathroom. Used the bathroom and I come out.
There was two beds there in the room and we were sleeping in the
one next to the door, so I just put myself on the one next to the
bathroom. I couldn't pull myself up to get blankets to cover up with,
and the longer I laid there, the more I got nailed to it. It was like I
was just glued to the bed. Couldn't move. So, I tried to call her.
Couldn't talk. I could just mumble a little bit. I could wave one hand
and kept mumbling. She'd been up all day and she was dead to the

world. I had a hard time waking her up. So, I kept mumbling. I got cold laying there.

Finally she come to. I'd left the light on in the bathroom and it lit up the room. She wanted to know what's the trouble. There's something wrong with you.

I'm all right, just trying to get covered up.

No. She called the front desk. Gee, within a minute these two security men came and called an ambulance, and within five minutes it was there. They took me down to the trauma center. It was around one o'clock. They hooked me up to pins and needles and shots. There was a speech therapist. She kept making me move my tongue, try to whistle, she'd take hold of it, pull it and try to make me roll my tongue, my cheek and all that. She came back about every hour for about 15 minutes and worked on it. She left at six o'clock. They got an ambulance to take me to Boston General Hospital. That was about 7:30. She drove up there and backed me in there and nobody seemed to get me. Then they came to get me and took me in. The ambulance guy had a clipboard with papers on it. When the nurse comes, just give her this, he said.

A woman came by, picked up the clipboard and she walked right along fast. Finally, two nurses came down and they were crying. I thought, my God, I'm in bad shape. They took me up the elevator, put me in the corridor and just left me there. There was nothing going on. A black woman came along and she was crying. She said, It's awful, it's awful, awful.

She kept talking and finally she said, You don't know what's going on, do you?

No. She went over and turned the TV on and that's when the plane was getting into Pennsylvania. They were all crying because that plane left Boston and they put a block on the city buildings and closed them up. They were getting as many doctors and nurses as they could possibly get to take to New York. All this stuff was going on while I was in there. I spent all that time frigging around there. Quite a spectacle. All this time I thought it was me that the fuss was about. They told me I had a stroke. The next morning the head doctor came in and said, You've had a massive stroke and you'll be lucky if you'll be able to walk. But not to count on it too much.

Mary left on Friday. They told me that the insurance wouldn't pay to move me over a radius of 60 miles. I thought I was going to have to stay in Massachusetts. The social worker came to see me and asked if there was anything she could do for me. I told her they were going to take me to New Hampshire or Massachusetts for rehab. I said, I want to go home.

Of course, you want to go home.

They told me I can't.

Aha, I'll see.

I called Mary. She wasn't at Toni's yet. She came back about an hour later.

MARY: He told me he was going to be leaving at 6:30 in the morning for Van Buren by ambulance. That was pretty good. They wouldn't let me take him. If you go out on your own, the insurance wouldn't pay for it.

BOB: The bed was about two feet wide. Wasn't as long as this table. Jesus Christ. My feet hung off over that. They were good. They were young. I wanted to sit up, so one of them pulled me and let me sit up for a little bit. My legs and ankles were so swollen from hanging off over that table.

Never had pain. I didn't have a blood clot. They don't know what it was, but they think a piece of cholesterol broke off, went up and killed that part of the brain, and it had to be retrained. The doctor said, It depends on how good the brain picks up the retraining.

But I come fast! I went up to Van Buren. My God, they work up there and I come fast. I come just so far and that was it. Couldn't come no further.

MARY: It's an excellent rehab place. When you don't improve anymore, that's when they ship you out.

BOB: I was there not quite three months. They let me come for an overnight and checked the house. They let me come home for Thanksgiving.

MARY: They told me everything I had to do to make it handicapped accessible. The first thing we did was pick up all the scatter rugs and move the furniture. I got rid of pretty much everything.

The stroke didn't take his memory. Or his mouth.

Chapter Eleven

Sharon: Firstborn

*We had to go to church. When Grampy was ready, you had to
do what he wanted to do. That's the way he was.*
    ~Sharon

SHARON: Grampy and I were working at the potato house.
Everyone was there and they'd gone home to get some more potatoes. It was time for church and Grampy always went to church on
Saturday night. It was four o'clock and I was the only one there with
him, so he made me go. We were all dirty and grumpy and I didn't
want to go. He said, I'm not running you home, you got to go.
    I can't go, I don't have a hat.
    So, he took out his dirty handkerchief and plunked it on my
head. You're going into church. I thought, I'm not going in there. We
went in and sat in the last pew and I wouldn't go to communion. He
nudged me and I thought, no, I'm *not* going. I couldn't pay attention.
I remember being so mad at Grampy. I had to go to church all dirty
and we never did that. The worst thing was, I was afraid he'd take his
dirty handkerchief off my head, blow his nose, and put it back on!
We had to go to church. When Grampy was ready, you had to do
what he wanted to do. That's the way he was.

99

Sharon's wedding day at Holy Rosary Catholic Church

I was born in Connecticut but I can't remember that. I remember living in the trailer next to Grampy and Grammy's house. I remember them building the little house, and we lived with Grampy and Grammy for a while because they sold the trailer and the house wasn't quite ready to move into. I remember moving in and Dad working down there all the time—the saws and wood everywhere.

We had no furniture. Dad made beds, bureaus, and cupboards for the little house.

My sister Pat and my brother Roger and I are close in age. We fought a lot when we were younger, but we all get along fine now.

When I was in junior high, I had Bob Cyr for a teacher. He asked me if I was Bob and Mary Campbell's daughter. I said I was. He said, You have a big family, don't you?

I said, Yeah, eleven of us. And after class I went up to him and said in a low voice, Mom's pregnant again. I used to be shy in class. I hated talking in front of the kids. I'd get sick when we had to do those oral reports. I'd be right sick to my stomach. We'd have plays and I'd be fine during the rehearsal. During the actual thing, I'd get scared. Sometimes I couldn't talk, couldn't get the words to come out. I'd have to go get a glass of water while I'm doing it and make sure I had something to drink.

The Fire

I was married then and Barb was down staying the night with us. We had an awful time getting up there because of all the water and ice in the road. My husband's father come up with us and it took us an hour just to get up there. The fire trucks weren't even there then. His father was an electrician. He went out to shut the power off from the barn to the house. The barn was gone, but the house didn't burn. There was a yard in between. It was a big barn. The animals burned. It was awful. Dad tried getting them out. I wasn't up there when all that happened. Barb had a horse in there and she was quite upset about that. They said they were glad she was down to our place and not up there. That same night before the fire, I had left Jenny [my daughter] up there. Mom was watching her. When I went to pick her up, my car wouldn't start, so I took their car. It was the old station wagon. Dad said, Next time you borrow a vehicle, take the newest one, because the new one burned in the barn. It was a Mercury Marquis. Everything was in there.

⟹◆⟸

SHARON: Us older kids had a different life than the ones that lived in town. Completely different. Sometimes comments were made because we always had to work out in the fields out on the farm and they never had to. They got to play basketball and all this. We always dreamed of doing that, but we could never find a way to town. Then we had to come home and work. It never bothered me, but I was grown up and gone by the time they moved. There's always good with the bad, no matter what.

My brother Roger was always real good with the kids all along. He takes them camping. Every summer he has taken my brothers and nephews on a fishing trip. Then the girls got mad. We started renting a camp so the girls could go, because it was too hard for Roger to take that many, and he had to have enough adults with him. He rented seven canoes once, one of the last times they went down the river. Four of my brothers went. I took Terry [my husband] up later. They got rained out and spent the night in the Haley potato house. It was the last day of the trip and I wasn't supposed to tell anybody they were near home, because a lot of the mothers [Sherrill] had let their little boys go. Ethan [Toni K.'s son] went later with his father Jim on a river trip. Terry had to work, and we were going to meet them near the end of the trip. They were out of a lot of food, so I went to town and got them beer, cookies, and soda. Then I met them at another spot. There had been a big egg fight from one canoe to another, so they had gone through all the eggs. It started raining, so they hurried

Jennifer [Sharon's oldest child] and Jacob [Jennifer's son]

and came down through. The boys didn't want to go home because they knew there was another day. Roger and Andy were farming together then. They went up to McGlinns' potato house and stayed there. We rented a camp at Long Lake once and took all the nieces and nephews.

BRENT [SHARON'S SON]: Roger got married and moved away. There are over 20 of us now, so it's hard to get all of us together.

LORI [SHARON'S DAUGHTER]: Roger started doing things with the boys and the girls got jealous, so every year the girls would go down to Bangor shopping.

SHARON: We used to spend a week or two at Grampie and Grammie Guerrette's camp on Mud Lake at the end of the summer after we picked rocks. Sometimes just the boys went, sometimes just the girls. Lots of times it was all of us. We had the tractor tire tubes. They had everything for us. We always loved going up there. Grammie's cooking was different than Mom's. We were in the lake the whole time we were there. They were always real nice to us. We didn't know their relatives that well. They talked French and we didn't know French. We knew their faces but we didn't know who they were or what they were saying. We'd go to the store and get an ice cream. It was different and was new territory for us. Dad always made sure we got a special week up there. We had sugar beets and we had to make sure all the mustard

103

Randy and Lori (Perreault) Leavitt

was pulled. That was worse than picking rocks—pulling mustard. You'd get all done and then you'd have to start all over again.

My brother Jim went to school at the convent. When we moved to the Ashby place, whoever was in public school went to Presque Isle. Whoever was at Holy Rosary went to Caribou. We had two buses stop in there and people used to make fun. So many kids needed two buses.

SHARON: Jim remembers the nuns were so mean.

JIM: Yes, the tallest one. But not Sister Rose. Terry went to Holy Rosary and was always in trouble, so then he went to Hilltop School.

SHARON: I had Sister Yvette, Grampie Guerrette's sister, in second grade, and that was the year when John Kennedy got shot. I remember her coming in and telling us, and they brought the TV in the rooms. We never had that much. They were all quite upset about it and you didn't see the nuns get like that very often.

When we worked on the Price farm, Dad owned it. Dr. Price had a ski tow for his kids, but he used Dad's farm truck to run it.

Dad used to keep it going for him because he wasn't always home. We got to go down there and go skiing. We'd take the Skidoo and pull ourselves up and we had toboggans. We had stuff to do all winter. We went up for hot chocolate. Uncle Tom would go up with us, Hubert, the neighbors, and the Prices would come up.

JIM: Even if the Prices weren't home we could still go down and use the ski tow.

SHARON: The Haleys lived next door. They were a little bit older and they'd come over and help us because sometimes we'd mess up the ski tow. We had wooden skis with jar rubbers on our boots. We put bread bags in our boots to keep our feet from getting cold.

We loved Grammy Campbell. My sister Pat and I spent the night up there a couple times a week and we had to eat what they had. And when they had liver, we'd send Roger that night.

JIM: We used to help watch Grammy Campbell when she got old.

SHARON: At Grampy Campbell's there was a smoldering fire in the cellar. [My daughter] Jessica called me at MFX [Maine Farmers Exchange] and said there was smoke, so I told her to hang up, go get the kids up, go to Roland and Steffie's because they were all home sleeping. I said, I need to get home, so one of the guys at work called the fire station for me.

Bud Haley said, I'll get you there.

We went and jumped in his car. There were cars coming and we went up the sidewalks and people were walking. I don't know how we missed some telephone poles. We were there, I'll bet, in five minutes, before Dad got there. Terry was in Mitchell's working. I called him before I left and we got there before Terry and the fire trucks. Hubert Haley was just pulling in. Hubert and Bud Haley are related to us. Bud was rough. Everybody knew Bud. Bud said, I don't care if there's cops out there, they can wait until I get to your house.

Bud had a pet bear for a couple of years. He'd take it in his car. He'd reach over and slap that thing and it'd slap him back. He's very impatient. He wouldn't sit and wait. He'd take his wife or others out to eat. When he was done, he got up and was gone. You'd better get up and go whether you were done eating or not. He wouldn't say anything, just go. You go if you want a ride. Everyone in all the restaurants knew him because they went out to eat a lot.

JENNY: Jacob and I ate at the Village one day and I went up to pay my bill and he had paid it.

SHARON: I am a secretary at MFX; I answer the phones and run orders.

JENNY: The place would fall apart without her. She takes her vacations in afternoons because if she were to take a week off, they'd call her every day.

Sharon and Uncle Roland

SHARON: If you take a vacation, you still have to call in. If you wanted more than two weeks off and they get along without you for more than two weeks, they didn't need you. That was their philosophy.

When Bud worked at MFX, he took the pickup in to get the brakes fixed at Midas in Caribou. He thought his wife was supposed to pick him up. I don't know if he didn't tell her or what, but she wasn't there to

Sharon and Tina

pick him up, and it was raining. He was so ugly, he walked home. Everybody knows him and tried to give him a ride. His grandsons tried to pick him up and he wouldn't take a ride. When he got home, he had blisters on his feet from walking in the rain, soaking wet. He was so mad but he wouldn't wait. He wouldn't take any rides because Rita was supposed to go pick him up. And she heard about it. It turned out that one of the guys at work was supposed to pick him up but Bud had in his mind that she was supposed to.

He had to be up in the morning. He and Tib were at work at five every morning, getting the trucks going, taking truckers where they were supposed to go.

BOB: Even after he was 70 years old, he was walking and walking, up and down the streets. He must be 90 by now.

107

JENNY: I loved the ice cream truck—Pete! It was white with blue lettering. We used to go on the ice cream truck. It was an old truck and it was really hard to drive. We bought the ice cream in Presque Isle, ice cream sandwiches, Popsicles, and Choco Tacos. I went with Joan and I sat with my feet up in the dashboard. The compressor was in the front seat, and there was only room for one person.

JESSICA: We always got free ice cream out of it, but we had to work for it. One time the ice cream truck was broke down on the Limestone Road and they couldn't find them—Joan and Jenny. I've never seen Dad so worried in all my life. Everybody and the cops were out on a big search. They had the money. The GIs were up there and all. They got a ride with somebody.

JIM: The guys had to go after that.

LORI: We played at Grampy and Grammy's on that hill and upstairs a lot.

JENNY: Whenever we spent the night with them, Grampy would make us scratch his back with a comb. We combed his hair.

TINA: We liked to do it.

JENNY: If it was Jessica and I, he'd send us with money to stock up on soda and candy because Mom never really let us have a lot of candy.

JENNY: I had my license and drove to school, so the others had me pick up stuff for them. Mom wouldn't buy candy unless it was a special occasion.

TINA: Roger would take us five kids to Flo's Inn and we'd always get soda and bubblegum. We had to work and have our own money.

Sharon's five children b: Jennifer, Jessica, Tina
f: Brent, Lori

LORI: If we wanted to be in sports, we had to make our own money to buy sneakers and go on trips.

SHARON: I'd buy them sneakers and clothes, but if they wanted that different stuff like the kids downtown, they had to earn their own money. Jessica had to have the brand-name stuff.

JESSICA: I babysat every weekend to make enough money for them.

Five generations!
b: Sharon, Jennifer, Mary
f: Mémère, Jacob

Campground

SHARON: When we lived up to the little house there was a brook down below, and Grampy Campbell fixed it all up in this really nice picnic area. Us girls had a tent and he made the boys a teepee, just like the Indians. We slept in there. Every night we camped down there. We wouldn't come home. We'd take our bath in the brook and we wouldn't go home during the summer. Grampy'd stay down there and watch us. We had family picnics.

JIM: Grampy made a bridge with digger lags nailed to poles.

SHARON: There was a railing, and you could see the brook when you walked across.

JIM: We got tarps for the teepee and fertilizer bags made of mesh nylon. We had a two-seater outhouse. Grampy used to come down to where we camped and try to scare us, make believe he was a bear.

SHARON: Well, us girls never got scared. Roger would get scared. He was a scaredy-cat. We'd go farther downriver and make houses out of branches, dam up the water, so the boys didn't get water for themselves. They'd bring hot dogs. The boys had their own and the girls had their own separate areas. We had a bridge.

JENNY: After our trailer burned and we moved up to Grampy Campbell's, we went down and played down there, catching salamanders and spiders.

SHARON: We weren't allowed near the well or near the big brook where they got spray water.

JIM: It had spray water in it.

SHARON: We drank the water and cooked with it. We picked berries, different kinds different times of the year—strawberries, raspberries, blueberries, and currants.

111

Uncle Roland and Aunt Steffie

SHARON: Uncle Roland and Steffie were always real good to the kids. Grampy and Uncle Roland never got along. They always said Roland was Grammy's boy. He was a mama's boy. He went off to the war—the army—got married and divorced. He has four children [Lona, Wendell, Joseph, Theresa] with his first wife [Evelyn] and he came up and started farming with Dad. He married Steffie and they had a boy [James Vincent] together. She was good with everybody. I remember one Christmas, I think we were living with Grampy and Grammy, Roland come up and had this great big box. It was right full of toys, and there was something for every one of us. He didn't have names or know what was what. He brought it in and we had a blast.

TINA: Great-Uncle Roland put a trailer out back where we used to have our family picnics and that was a camp. It was back in the woods. We all used to spend the night up there. We kept it mowed and made sure everything was going. Roland enjoyed being outside so he sat outside. Even when he was sick with cancer, he'd sit on the porch. He only came in at 11:00 to watch *The Price is Right* and to eat lunch. At five he came in to eat supper and watch the news, and it was always boring. It was always real loud. That was the only time he watched the boob tube. That's what he called it.

JENNY: Uncle Roland and Steffie babysat us. If we cried, he'd say, Is that necessary? Now is that necessary? Okay, you kids go outside and get the stink blown off ya.

SHARON: If the kids had ear infections, Roland smoked a pipe and he'd blow smoke in their ears. I worried about it, but Dr. Hayward used to tell us, Hey, if it works, don't stop doing it. And it melts the wax. But the smoke did stop them from crying, so they could get their medicine.

JENNY: And our hot toddies.

SHARON: I was so glad to have Dr. Hayward for all the kids.

TINA: Uncle Roland used to do a lot of stuff with us. He used to have chickens.

JENNY: We'd get the eggs and the chickens would peck at our sneakers. He hung the chickens to chop their heads off. One time the chicken fell to the ground and was still walking around with its head chopped off, and it ran in front of us.

LORI: He'd chop the heads off and they'd still run around.

JIM: Even with their heads cut off, they'd jump right at you— high. He'd do 100 every year.

JENNY: He got us ducks one year. We were scared of them, so we gave them to Roger because he had a pond.

Jessica and Abbigail [Sharon's daughter and granddaughter]

Anne Guerrette and Brent [Sharon's son]

SHARON: Then when the kids found out Roland killed the chicken, they wouldn't eat chicken. They'd only eat store-bought chicken. They'd help Steffie take the feathers off and that didn't bother them, but chopping the heads off did.

After we moved here we had a tent for the kids and their friends to camp out. Nothing like what we used to. When one had a friend out to play, the others always wanted to have a friend, too. It wasn't fair for one and not the other. So, we'd have double the trouble there.

⇒◆⇐

I've told Roger, I'm so lucky, because all my family comes and they know everybody, not just Terry and I, and stay with everybody and they're comfortable going with them.

JENNY: Uncle Roger always came down and did stuff with us when Dad was gone driving truck, too. He'd try to make us eat stuff like partridge. He lied to us one day. They had gotten a moose and told us it was regular hamburger and it was really moose. It tasted different and we all knew.

SHARON: If Steffie was away, Roger's first wife, Doreen, babysat. We always ate great big meals—meat and potatoes—and Doreen would just have a sandwich. They were always starving when they got home. She had two boys and they ate good, but our kids ate more than normal kids. I always made a shepherd's pie or a casserole and took for her to have for dinner [noon meal]. What we called snacks, she'd have for lunch. Sandwiches and cookies were our snack. I'd hear all about it when they got home, because they could only have one hot dog. I would take enough so they could all eat. Then they said Roger ate it all, that they didn't get hardly any.

I used to feel guilty when I'd go into town. I didn't take them all shopping with me. They took turns going downtown. I'd only take one or two at a time, but they didn't know how to cross the street and they didn't know how to make change. So, then I thought, I'll have to make them start doing it. I think to this day Brent still throws all his money down and lets the cashier count out what she needs. I had a hard time with him.

JESSICA: He should have worked on the ice cream truck, so he could learn how to make change.

SHARON: Kids downtown were street-smart. My kids weren't. They trusted everybody and talked to everybody. They were always around big dogs and animals and there are nasty dogs and nasty animals.

Mom and Dad, they don't just worry about us kids. They still check up on us kids and all their grandchildren too, and they know everything going on. They try to go to all their functions at school.

Toni K.: The kids couldn't get away with anything because it's on Grampy's scanner.

Sharon: There was always somebody watching. They always knew what we did before we got home.

Lori: After Grampy and Grammy won the Megabucks, they got a time-share at a resort in Island Falls. Every year they would invite everybody down for a week. We went canoeing and hiking. We had scavenger hunts. We went to Horn of Plenty restaurant. They still go there.

Jenny: I'd take a week off from work to go there.

<hr />

Sharon: I was told not to have any more children after the third. Then I got pregnant while I was on the pill and had Brent. Then I got pregnant with Lori after Terry had a vasectomy. Brent teased Lori.

Lori: He'd swat me across the head and say, You're a mistake! I got smart enough to say, I'm a miracle.

Sharon: I had five kids and I finally got to be an aunt. It was Jason.

After us girls started having our weekends going to Bangor shopping, the boys went to Canada or had a night out. My brother Mike doesn't drink and he was always the designated driver. They had a few escapades. One time when they came back from Canada and got to the border, Roger got them in trouble. The Border Patrol asked where they lived and he said in a house. Then he said a green house. One time they searched the car. Sometimes my sisters were a bad influence on my kids. They used to go to Canada because you could drink over there and you couldn't over here. My girls started going with my sisters. At the time, the drinking age was 18 there and 21 here.

l–r: Ann, Mary, Toni K., Barbara, Pat, Janelle, Sharon, Jennifer, Jessica, Joan, Tina, Lori, Roberta

JENNY: Janet and Kim took me for my 18th birthday.

SHARON: I knew they were going.

The 13 of us never had curfews. We just had to be able to get up in the morning and go to work. If you couldn't, then you were in trouble. You had to be home and be in bed at eight o'clock. But if you could stay out all night and get up the next morning and go to work, that was fine. Make it to school or whatever. Dad always made us eat healthy. He always had a cow and we had meat and potatoes and ate big meals, so we wouldn't have to go to the doctors so much. We had to dress up and wear ski pants. No one else wore ski pants in high school. The younger kids did. Dad made us wear ski pants. We would go outside in the woodshed and change while we

117

b: Tina, Jennifer, Sharon, Terry, Jessica
f: Lori and Brent

waited for the bus or we'd change on the bus. He looked and he
caught on and he locked us out of the house one night. We got home
and the doors were locked and he said, You want to go without ski
pants, you stay out there without ski pants. That's when minidresses
were coming too, and we had fights over that. There was Pat, Barb,
and me. We all tried different ways. Roger used to get into trouble.
If someone did something wrong we'd all get punished. I used to feel
bad. Roger would get the brunt of it a lot of times because he was
the oldest boy. Once I went off the road and Roger was with me. It
was in the middle of the winter and Dad made him ride in the back
of the pickup. Here I was the one driving.

When my kids were all home I wouldn't answer the phone
because it was never for me. They were only allowed to talk five
minutes. Then they had to hang up and no one calls after eight
o'clock. They'd say, No one else is like that.

I put my foot down. Terry was on the road driving truck and he'd try to call and he couldn't get through. I told them if they had that much to talk about they could write a letter. They were going to see them the next day at school anyway. I'd get them a piece of paper and pen. I'd take the phone and tell them goodbye to whoever it was. They all knew and they were all really good about it. They respected. Even their friends all knew, too. Once in a while their friends would call after eight and I'd answer the phone. They'd apologize because they knew. We're so sorry. We didn't realize the time. I expected some of them to be rude but they were all nice, never gave me a hard time. I'm sure they said other things but not to my face.

TINA: That's just the way it was. Even now at our house and it's after eight and the phone rings, I say, Who's calling this time of night? There was a broom closet in our kitchen and our phone was right on that wall. So, whenever we'd talk to our friends we'd wrap ourselves around in the cord, go in that closet, and talk to our friends—for five minutes.

SHARON: When we moved up to the old house, Hubert Haley was our neighbor. We used to play and go to school with their kids. They had a dog, Brownie. They loved that dog, but we'd get off the bus and that dog'd run to our house. Hubert'd have to come up and get it. He did that for about a month and he kept getting stronger chains and the dog kept breaking them. Whatever he did, the dog kept breaking it, cry and go it, and he ended up at our house. Finally he said, I may as well let you guys have him because he's always up here. So, we kept him. He could still come up and see him because he came up to visit a lot. So, we got a dog from Hubert and he always came to check on him.

One Halloween my car wouldn't start and we hadn't gotten down there for Halloween. They always went out trick-or-treating. He called and thought something was wrong. I told him my car wouldn't start.

Thirteen *is* a Lucky Number

We were waiting for Terry to get home. It was getting late, so Hubert came up and took them trick-or-treating to make sure they got out.

Once Jenny was walking after school. There was something going on at the Armory and I let her stay after school. Terry's best friend called me at work and said, Did you know that Jennifer's downtown walking in the street? I couldn't imagine you letting her downtown.

I told him I gave her permission. Everybody watches for them. I always know what they're doing.

The reason it got less strict was when Terry stayed home. They had their father wrapped around their little fingers.

Tina: When he told us not to do something we'd go *hmmmmm*. With Mom we'd give it a couple of times before she'd go *aghhhhh*. They'd ground us and Dad'd say we were grounded forever and two days later we wouldn't bring it up.

Jim: Our father [Bob Campbell] stuck to what he said. But we figured that out. We outnumbered him, so when he got mad and said he'd kick our ass up to our heads, we'd take off running in different directions, and whoever he caught, got in trouble. I was on the track team. I could run fast. I was third in the state.

Sharon: We'd argue and get in fights and Dad would throw us outside. He bought us boxing gloves. He'd make us put them on and we'd have to go outside and box it out. So, we couldn't come in the house and fight. You want to fight? That's fine, but you do it outside with the boxing gloves, fair and square.

Jim: Roger was playing around one time. He picked me up and threw me through a wall. Didn't take him long to fix though.

Sharon: I remember Pat and Roger got in a fight. Roger ripped his shirt off and threw it at her. Then you never knew what the fights were about.

Once when we kids were alone they were climbing in the big barn. It had inner walls. They were up there doing something, I don't

Luke and Tina (Perreault) Moir

know what. Roger fell through and got his arm caught in a nail and it ripped all the way down. I was taking a bath and they came in hollering, Roger cut his arm off! Mom and Dad weren't home. Pat didn't want him to use a white towel. She took it away because she did the laundry and she wouldn't let him get it dirty. I came down and saw his arm. I said, Your arm is still there. They were all crying. He had to have it stitched, the muscle part and everything.

Brent and Jason were working picking rocks for Roger. He had some older boys from Parker Siding working, too. They were picking on Brent and Jason because they were younger. Roger was harder on them because they were family. He always gave in to the others because Brent and Jason would complain to him. He'd tell them to toughen up or put up with it. Those older guys made Brent go down and fill up their water jugs at the brook. Brent peed in it and brought it back. They drank it. Roger found out. Brent said he got even with them.

The kids sucked their thumbs or their fingers when they were little. My Grampy tried to break them of the habit. They tried everything to get some of them to quit. I'm glad I never did. I saw Roger once going to get his thumb cut off. Grampy'd take his jack-knife right out to cut. He'd have the jackknife right there and they'd be screeching and hollering. We'd be so scared that Grampy'd do that. We still sucked them. We just didn't do it in front of Grampy.

At home we couldn't talk on the phone. We were never allowed to get calls. It was for people to call, not for you to use. It was emergencies and business. If Dad lost a load of potatoes because we were on the phone! He wasn't going to have that happen. We didn't have a phone at the little house. We would walk down and use Grammy's.

No jobs were girls' or boys'. The girls had to work in the potato house and the boys had to do dishes. We all had to do whatever, take our turn at cooking the meals. Mom was always in the potato house too, or the field. Mom told Barb to cook cabbage and she cooked lettuce.

It was fall and Terry was working at the farm. Dad always wanted them all to have the trucks filled with fuel before they left. Terry was under the boom and ran out of fuel. Dad went up one side of him and down the other. Terry tried to explain that someone else had that truck in town and that he didn't fill it up. That wasn't the one he filled up. But they still talk about that, and to this day it's a bad subject to mention between the two of them.

TERRY: He means well. Even after he and Mary got in that bad accident and he had a bad back, as bad as we got along, I put him in the truck with me and gave him $300 a week to help get by. He used to go to Texas with me.

SHARON: Dad had his Class 1 license. Terry had a new Peterbilt and he'd drive all the time to make the payments. He'd take Dad, so he could log the books. He drove, according to the logging records. Roland worked for him and drove, too.

JENNY: I drove! I drove the Peterbilt.

TERRY: She was 12 years old and she drove back from Bangor. I'd get up there by Howland. The seats were close together, so I just scooted over and I said, Jennifer, go ahead and drive. She was driving right along and I'd set the cruise control. We were driving up the road. Another McCain truck passed me and they looked over and said, Damn, McCain, you sure start them out pretty young, don't ya? If there's all kinds of room aboard, they got to start out young.

SHARON: Terry didn't like taking the girls on long hauls because he couldn't go to the bathroom with them. They'd go on the short trips in Maine. Brent got to go out in the mines. He was really young. They went to Kansas City, Nebraska, Chicago, and Florida. When Terry got home he said, All that kid eats is hot dogs the whole time.

Jessica (Perreault) and Travis Robbins

TERRY: We put 27,000 miles on the truck before we got home. I told Sharon, You know what? It's going to be a long time before he says, Dad, let's get in the truck and go. The telephone rang about 20 minutes later. It was McCain's and they said, Can you be in Indianapolis in two days?

I said, Yeah, and Brent said, Dad, can I go? It was summertime break. I still drive truck once in a while. I went to work for Maine Military Authority (Jim, Dave, Lance, and Travis also work there) and worked as a mechanic. Then when they wanted to start trucking their own equipment, I did that for five years. And now I'm in the shop trying to fall into a supervisor job, so I don't have to be on the road. I buy trucks and sell them to farmers.

SHARON: To irritate me. It ties up a lot of money and room in the garage.

TERRY: I do family repairs, too. From four to eight at night I can get a lot done.

SHARON: Terry and I went to school together. We've always known each other and worked together. Terry was working for Hubert Haley at the time. I was babysitting John and Nancy Haley's daughter, Jennifer. Terry came to fill the pickup with gas after dark one night when I was there. I thought someone was stealing gas, so I went to check on it. And that was when he asked me out.

CHAPTER TWELVE

Sunday Afternoon at Bob and Mary's

That's when we had the best food because Mom would buy us
Devil Dogs and soda. We never had candy or soda any other
time of the year.
         ~Pat

JOAN: I played basketball with Bert [Roberta] and Janet and
then Kim and Janet. I was the middle one.

Wayne Knight was the radio announcer for the basketball
games. He could actually say our names right—Camp-*bell*.

The coach Jeannette Peters retired when she was done with the
Campbells. We took summer trips where Mr. Peters's mother lived
in Eastport. He was driving and we had a tire blow out in Dad's blue
van. It was loud. So, we pulled into an old gas station and it had
antique gas tanks. Ken [Mr. Peters] backed over the gas tank. The van
was packed full with all the tents and coolers. We had to unpack
everything to get to the jack. We tented out at campgrounds and
played other teams to get experience. That was a lot of fun.

Bert is the only one who went to basketball camp in Connecticut.
She was the best player. She's as tall as Kim. Bert even made a basket
for the other team once. She was so proud and everyone was hollering.
She made up for it by making that basket from half court.

BOB: She went to college at University of Maine to play ball. She lasted a month. It was too much. She had to be on the floor, not in the classroom, and she couldn't keep up. She was taking mechanical engineering. She quit and went to Georgia.

MARY: Joan was more timid.

JOAN: Janet played the outside court. I was either on and would make every basket or would never make one. We could read each other well. Kim was more klutzy.

MARY: Kim always had to make sure how she looked. She was so skinny and her arms were so long. She was just everywhere. Like a tree.

PAT: One advantage of a big family is that for us older ones, we had younger ones to babysit when we started having kids. There's thirty years' difference between the oldest and youngest grandchild.

MARY: We used to plan everything around church. We had no choice; we had to go to church.

PAT: We had to change out of our church clothes when we got home from church. We had to wear dresses to Holy Rosary and had to change out when we got home. On the bus we were called the Holy Rollers because we carried big book bags to the Holy Rosary Parochial School. None of the other schoolkids did.

I confessed to Mom last week that I hadn't been going to church. We just don't have time anymore. It seems like it's the only time we have to run the roads. Now with the 11 o'clock service, your day is gone.

KIM: I cried to go and I went only one day to the convent school with Barb on the bus. It might have been the last day of school.

PAT: Sharon made Kim a dress out of red border print fabric to wear that special day. I still have that fabric in a box. It was red and white and had little hearts on it.

MARY: Sharon was very artistic.

PAT: She never used a pattern. She'd chop up fabric and make dresses.

MARY: Remember that dress I got her for eighth grade graduation? She needed a dress to go somewhere. She took that dress all apart. It was a two-piece outfit. I couldn't believe it. I paid a lot of money for it at Penney's. She wanted something to wear. She fixed it, put it back together, and had a new outfit. And she wore it.

———⟫·◇·⟪———

I'll bet [Michael's wife] Mary will tell you she's the favorite daughter-in-law because she's Mary M. Campbell and so am I.

———⟫·◇·⟪———

Ann Nicole [Pat's daughter]

WAYNE [PATRICIA'S HUS-BAND]: I remember coming in the front door (of the Campbell house) because I had to change the time of our date. I saw all the little girls lined up on the staircase peeping around the corner.

PAT: He came to the front door. So, they were all going to see who came to the front door.

WAYNE: I didn't know not to go to the front door. I should tell you how I met Pat. I worked at the NCO [Noncommissioned Officers] Club part-time. The

Ben, Pat, Wayne, Andy and Ann

job as a security policeman didn't keep me busy enough. I had to wear this frilly shirt with a vest. You had to order the frilly shirt, like the old tuxedo, only it came with ruffles on the sleeves. I wasn't going to wear a ruffled-sleeved shirt, so I took it to the men's store that I ordered it from. Usually they write out a ticket and send it across the street to their seamstress. Well, this time, for some reason, they gave me the ticket and the shirt and said, Take it over there.

Another redhead. That's where I met Pat.

PAT: I altered him. Both ways.

He came back the second time on Friday the 13th and asked if I'd do stripes on the sleeve. I said I'd never done it before but probably could, so he came back the next day, Saturday.

Would you like to go out for dinner? he said.

128

I'm sitting there thinking, oh, my God, I work during dinner on Monday. How am I going to tell him, No I'm not available for dinner. I said, What time?

Then he said, Six o'clock.

I think, okay. Supper, not dinner. I thought it was noontime dinner.

WAYNE: I got promoted. Prior to that I sewed my own stripes.

PAT: I've done it ever since.

WAYNE: We met on Friday the 13th. She's one of 13 children. We bought our first home on July 13th at 1300 in the afternoon. We bought our second house on July 13, 1998. It seems like that 13 keeps coming up.

PAT: I had appendicitis on July 13th.

WAYNE: I retired from the Air Force in 1998 with 22 years and 10 months. I went back to school for three years. Did work study and odd jobs. That's how I met Bob O'Brien. I worked on his gardens for two years. Our first two sons were born here at Loring. We lived in one of Sharon's trailers for a while until we got into base

Pat, Emily and Wayne

housing. It was so cold; we hung a tapestry on the windows to keep the wind from blowing through. The kitchen table came from the A-frame that Terry's uncle built. We got a set of chairs from her aunt Loretta and Pat re-covered them. We got a vinyl, outdoor love seat off the porch from Vick and Verna Perreault. We borrowed a coffee table and a black-and-white TV.

PAT: We got married in October, so for our first Christmas, we used gum wrapper chains to wrap the tree. We hung his Matchbox cars on the tree, strung popcorn, and made pipe-cleaner candy canes. Then my brother turned around and gave us a dog for Christmas.

WAYNE: There was the son-in-law briefing. Robert would pull us aside, and I don't know if it was before we actually got married or not.

PAT: It wasn't so much that he pulled you aside; we just left you there with him. We knew what was going to happen.

WAYNE: We got the whole story—his philosophy of life and being able to work in The County: you don't have to go outside The County to find work. We learned Bob Campbell very well.

PAT: I remember when Bert brought David home that one time. David got stuck out on the porch with Dad, and we all come in here, laughing. Ha ha, he's getting the lecture. We called it "the initiation."

BOB: I told the new son-in-law that I believe in The County. I believe that families should stay together where they are. I don't believe in everybody and all these nationalities getting together. I tell them a person can make a living in their own hometown. If they can't, they can't make it out of town. There's where they got to be. All they have to do is smarten themselves up and do it. There's rich people in every town and there's poor people in every town, so you just make up your mind what you want to be, and you got to do it. You just can't sit back and let it come to you. You bring your family up there so they know their uncle.

PAT: Dad would talk and talk. They were too new to the family to be rude and get up and leave. He just would tell all his stories. You don't get up and leave even if you'd heard them before.

WAYNE: You come into a family function now and there are the new girlfriends, boyfriends that come with the nephews and nieces. The first thing they do is look at all the people. They sit in the corners. The first time my son-in-law Lance came, he got upset and sick to his stomach.

BOB: I told all the grandsons as soon as they grew up: You go out and you pick up a woman. You want to go to the VFW and get one and get a good one. Pick them out if they're strong. If you want to find out if she's the woman for ya, you give her a round-pointed shovel and tell her to dig a ditch four feet deep and a hundred feet long. If she gets that all dug you say, Okay, come right back in the house. If she says, Why? say, I just wanted to see if you could do it. If she doesn't sass you or anything, well that's the woman you want to marry.

MARY: Poor Amber, that girl that came over with Anthony [Gary's son] and Bob said that to her. She didn't ever want to come back here again.

PAT: Mom would buy big bundles of bird's-eye cotton for diapers. She'd tear them off to the size they needed to be and Sharon and I would sit and hem. We rolled the edges and stitched. We used Grammy Campbell's sewing machine. I went from hemming diapers to sewing for 4-H: three-quarter scarves, our aprons that were gathered, and gathered skirts. You had to progress up for 4-H, and we had to enter them at the fair and do the dress review (4-H stands for hands, heart, head, and health). I sewed for my mother.

WAYNE: Mary and Pat were teaching sewing lessons at the Viking Sewing Center. Pat and I were dating. In order to spend a little time with her, I bought a sewing machine and she taught me how to sew. I made her a few things.

PAT: You made me a dress. I still have it, too.

WAYNE: She had a buyer for the sewing machine around her parents' 25th wedding anniversary, and we let them keep the money for that for our contribution toward the party. Pat has plenty of sewing machines.

PAT: Should I count them all? I have my two that I use all the time. I have two sergers, a featherweight, and the old treadle machine. I always did sewing on the side while the kids were growing up, mostly stripes and alterations. For a while, western shirts were popular with the guys going to the NCO Club, so I did several of those. I did a lot of costumes and some church banners. We helped with the school social studies class quilts. The kids tied them.

In 1985 the family bought me a ticket to come home from Texas for the basketball tournament. Wayne had our three kids to take care of during his finals. I told my sisters if they made it to the tournament, I'd come home to watch the big tournament. They lost! I jinxed them all.

MARY: When Jim came home from four years of being in the army, he was so scared he'd have to go back. He was a tank driver in the Fulda Gap in Germany, where they were so nervous, they were shooting each other.

PAT: Sharon was 16 and I was 15. We were driving the farm truck home from Arnold Haines's. Dad rented that farm. It was loaded full and Dad said, Girls, you take it back to the farm.

Sharon gets in and starts driving, and we're getting on Whitmore Hill. She couldn't get it shifted enough, so the dumb truck stalled. We started rolling back with a full load of potatoes. She's pushing on the brake. I'm yanking the emergency brake back as far as I can and I yelled at Sharon, Don't go in the ditch, don't go in the ditch!

I'm not!

She's trying to get it started. We never did get it started. We finally got to the low part where we stopped rolling and I just held onto that brake the whole time. She walked up to the house to call to get somebody to help us. I thought I was going to pull that emergency brake right out of the floor. Thankfully, nobody was behind us for us to roll back down that hill. She kept her on the road. Didn't roll down the ditch. Holy frig! That scared me to death. You can just tell when a motor's going to stall. I'm just dying. Oh, my God. Don't stall, don't stall, don't stall. I never drove truck after that. I would never learn how to drive truck. Sharon just got her license and he had her drive that truck home.

BOB: On the Price farm—that was steep. The oldest truck I had was a '51 GMC and I put a fertilizer body on it with the auger on the side. It was full of fertilizer and I sent Sharon up on top of the hill with that. It tipped and went way over here and all of a sudden, *whump!* It'd go back this way. It didn't have enough power and just barely got over. But she did it again. And she'd do it again.

PAT: I never drive. I had to drive standard with Wayne's little Toyota car when we met.

WAYNE: She got her cousin to go with her.

PAT: The only other standard we'd drive was the tractor. We took turns driving and picking rocks. Driving would be our break. You'd hit the clutch and your foot would slip off and you'd tear your shin. I hated that. You had to learn to get the right tension, so you wouldn't rip your shin. We all had shin dings, scars from the clutch.

Grampy Campbell had a campground down at the brook. That was always fun. It was nicer before the younger kids lived there. Grampy went down there and cleaned it up. He built a platform for us to have a tent on. The boys had the teepee. They used a truck canvas to make a teepee for the boys to sleep in on old mattresses.

We had an outhouse down there. You'd have to get up and go in the middle of the night. We made our own food but we ran home for breakfast. We'd pick berries—raspberries and strawberries to eat—and take our socks and shoes off and walk in the brook. It'd cramp your feet, it was so cold. It felt good, too.

BOB: I went down there one night and I growled and growled. Roger and Dave took off up to the house. Roger'd say, Come on, Dave. Come on. Dave'd turn around to see what was coming. Roger would just go. Dave'd go 10 or 12 feet and turn around. I'd growl and shake the tents. Dave thought it was something different, but Roger was sure it was a bear.

PAT: Roger, Sean [Joan's husband], and I tagged along and we went fishing down there. People had said there was a bear in that area. We were fishing. All of a sudden, Sean yells, A bear!

Roger threw his pole and was gone. There really was a bear there, but Roger didn't go back for his pole. Sean, at least, brought his pole. Good old days.

MARY: Roger was always timid that way. He wouldn't even wear a Halloween mask until he was eight or nine years old. Scared to death of Halloween.

⇒•◇•⇐

JOAN: On the farm we had to pick rocks. We got to walk behind the harvester and throw the potatoes that they missed into the next row. All the little girls did that.

MARY: Roberta mentioned picking mustard.

JOAN: We picked mustard for Red Smith in the sugar beet fields. We used to be queens—Mustard Queen—whoever had the biggest bouquet collected in our arms. We had to make our fun. It was boring otherwise. It's like picking rocks. You'd come across some rock you thought was so beautiful. You toted it around with you. By the time you got it home, it was dry. Why did I save that? And you'd pitch it.

Terry said that Red Smith was the best man he ever worked for. He told his crew if they got to work a half hour early in the morning, he'd cook them breakfast. He cooked a big breakfast of bacon and eggs, ham and toast. Then if the crew had to work late, he'd cook them supper, too.

BOB: We used to have around 175 acres to pick rocks.

MARY: Even after the mechanical rock pickers, we still had to pick rocks by hand.

JOAN: There was a lady at work saying that her mother used to give her family a choice: you can stay in and help me cook supper or you can go out and play. I said, We could either stay in and cook supper or go outside and work doing chores.

I always liked to stay in and help cook supper. Some of the others collected the eggs and we had three pigs.

PAT: Sharon and I didn't do much of that. When we got home from school we had to make the dessert. We always made cookies or cake. Then started peeling potatoes. Mom would do the meat because I couldn't do meat. Sharon, Barb, and I would take turns cooking lunch during harvest. We'd have a day off from working on the harvester. Mom would tell us what to fix for lunch because she had to go work the conveyors in the potato house. So, it was our day to stay inside and babysit. Mom told Barb to boil up some cabbage and do the potatoes, meat, and make a green salad. Instead, we come in and there was mush at the bottom of the pan for the cabbage. She took the head of lettuce and boiled that instead of the cabbage. We had the best laugh. Poor Barb.

Sharon and I used to stay overnight up at Grammy Campbell's Friday night. Then, we never wanted to eat Grampy Campbell's cooking because we didn't know what kind of meat he was using for the cooking. Partridge stews or whatever. We never dared to eat anything. Grampy would call it Mulligan Stew. They had headcheese. Oh, gosh, I'd cringe. We tried to go up after supper if we were going to stay overnight. She taught us how to play canasta and she'd have a jigsaw puzzle out. They'd have pancakes, beans, and home fries sometimes.

Bob and his favorite daughter, Joan

I remember getting home from school and Grampy always made us peanut butter and butter sandwiches. We never understood that. Wayne still does it that way. It's all lubricated that way. Grampy said it was to fatten us up.

BOB: My father used to say if Pat and Sharon lived to be five years old, you wouldn't be able to kill them with a gun.

PAT: It was fun at her house because they had a second step up with boot storage in there. Then she had the cupboard underneath the stairs where she stored the flour bin. Grammy'd be off at the other end of the house and we'd go in through that step and crawl through, out and around through. We used to have the best fun. Oh, we'd get sassed. Oh, it was so much fun.

BOB: My mother had candy that came in pails and she kept the pails. She had molasses donuts, sugar donuts, chocolate donuts, and then she had cinnamon rolls. And she made date cookies and date squares.

PAT: Grampy had the garden and we'd go in there and steal carrots out of the garden and go hide in the asparagus bush. There was a currant bush and we had to pick those.

<hr />

JOAN: Pete, the ice cream truck. That's how I learned to drive standard. I learned him right out here in the driveway—the H column. No power steering, no nothing. So, it would have been like the old Chevy farm truck. Dave still has Pete. He took the ice cream freezer off the truck. It all rotted out.

The first year I started doing it, I went with Bert. She always drove. We had the best time just driving to and from because it's a big steering wheel. We'd pretend it was really bumpy, and she bounced around and she would wave to everyone. It had a bell. At

b: Sean and Joan
f: Noah and Jonathan

first there was one on the floor but that wore out, so we hooked one up on the handle that you just pushed up and down.

Besides going around the base, we did the Limestone parade and we did a couple farmers' auctions, and The Lumberjack Roundup a few times. We went to the Northern Maine Fair in

Presque Isle one year and made big money at the tractor pull. But the fair association didn't get the money, so that didn't last.

I remember doing the tractor pull one night. I got done at about 11 o'clock at night. The alternator—something—was going in that engine. Trying to get that through town in Presque Isle. Luckily it stopped by the police station. Dad came over and drove. It had no lights, nothing. That was the bad thing about it. It did break down. You'd have to lift the hood and beat something with a wrench if it wouldn't start. I don't know exactly what it was. You'd go to a STOP at every little court on base. Then you'd go to start it. This little block thing, carburetor, you'd have to hit it with the wrench and try it again.

I ran out of gas one time on the way home. A guy that pulled off right behind figured something was going wrong, so he took me to DoDo's in Caribou to get gas. Well, I left the keys right in it. I put the money in the freezer and locked it. And Pam Obar came by and called home. She said the ice cream truck is there and nobody's with it. The keys are in it. That stirred things up. I was scared. After that I filled up every day. It didn't matter.

BOB: The kids over there at the base—it was just like going out in the woods and finding monkeys. They knew absolutely nothing. They'd come up to you with a great big jukebox on their shoulder, and they'd give you a 20-dollar bill and wanted to know if they had enough money to buy their buddy an ice cream. Then we'd get a call from the parents at the base. Did you find a certain coin? The kids'd steal their parents' coin collection.

MARY: One time it was Barb. They called Cyr Brothers because they knew that's where we got the ice cream. That's how they contacted us. Well, it was a Confederate two-dollar bill and these people had had it for years and years. We found it!

JOAN: Kids would follow us on their bikes to harass. And there were chains that you hooked to hold the tailgate up or down. So,

Sean and Joan

they'd grab the chains while you were driving. I'd slam on the brakes.

MARY: Sue came home one night from driving the ice cream truck and brought her stuff in. She didn't have the moneybag. Right before they left to come home they took all their empty boxes and threw them in the dumpster on base. She figured she must have dumped it out. She went back and they climbed in the dumpster and retrieved the moneybag.

BOB: It was a lot of work keeping up. We had to go to town, get the ice cream, bring it home and put it in the freezer.

PAT: I'd leave Presque Isle and I'd be here in seven minutes, so the ice cream wouldn't melt.

JOAN: I just took the truck to Cyr Brothers' and loaded it there.

MARY: I picked it up at Sure Winner Foods in Presque Isle.

PAT: We farmed and you [younger girls] worked on the ice cream truck. I'd rather farm.

JOAN: I think I would have, too, but it turned my hair blonde from being outside all the time. I have blonde hair for my senior picture.

BOB: Had to have something to keep them busy.

⊨⊹⊨

JOAN: The gate where Bert's lamb was kept wasn't good enough. The lamb got out and the chickens pecked it to death. We had to go bury it and it was muddy. We were heading down toward the rock pile and dragging him in a burlap bag. Bert was crying. We were laughing because we were getting stuck in the mud. Barb thought she was going to have to leave her leg there.

———⊰•◦•⊱———

JOAN: Dad took us trick-or-treating, so he could get something to eat. He'd go inside with us, especially at Carmen Campbell's. She always had pie for Dad. It would be on the tail end of the trip.

PAT: We couldn't believe it when we moved to Fort. Wow, all these houses. You'd go forever out in the country for ten houses. We got here and filled a bag just on the hill.

JOAN: We got to work for Dad on Lee Somers's farm and also for Herschel Smith.

b: Mike, Mary, Roger, David, Sharon, Brent, Bob
m: Sherrill, Jessica, Kim, Lori, Tina, Janet
f: Joan and Sean

Potato harvest in The County

PAT: That was the last year I worked on the harvester for you.

WAYNE: You're still working on the harvester.

MARY: For all the years you missed out on it.

PAT: I prefer working on the harvester to picking.

The girls were picking at Red Smith's. It was the end of the season and we went and picked on a Sunday to help out. The kids had gone back to school or something.

That was another fun thing—packing lunch for when we picked. Four loaves of bread. We packed the sandwiches right back in the bread bags. That's when we had the best food because Mom would buy us Devil Dogs and soda. We never had candy and soda any other time of the year. We'd get them for harvest though. Root-beer barrels and butterscotch hard candies. Lots of candy, sugar, and sweets. Got store-bought bread for sandwiches instead of homemade bread. We were all good pickers.

BOB: They were all good workers.

MARY: My sisters and I were all good pickers, too. Except Regina. She was younger.

JOAN: We had to buy our own basketball sneakers. They always took the orders at harvest time.

PAT: We never got money. We picked for Dad or worked for Dad on the harvester. Never got anything for the longest while until we found out kids in school get paid! What's the deal here? We don't get paid! Mom and Dad would say, You got clothes and all that. We buy you clothes. These other kids have to go buy clothes. At least we buy them for you. Well, yeah, I guess, but they get paid! There was still that concept. Hmmmm.

You got a roof over your head. There's food on the table.

That was always the hard part when you'd go back to school afterwards, and they'd ask how much you made during digging. They wanted you to fill out a paper for the survey. Like, none. Had to make up something, I don't know. A cruel reminder that we don't get paid.

I used to babysit. Got all kinds of money for that. Then I'd buy my M&M's and hide them in my dresser drawer, but the kids always knew they were there. I got a case of M&M's from my son Ben for Christmas.

JOAN: It was her favorite present.

Isn't that what sold her on the house? You didn't see them but Wayne did. There were M&M's in the cupboard.

I work at Defense Finance and Accounting Services. I dreamed last night that DFAS closed and I bought Mom's shop and opened a day care. A dream? It was a nightmare.

CHAPTER THIRTEEN

Roger: Oldest Son

It was my first true-blue Christmas: perfectly blue skies, clear blue water, and my first Christmas away from home.
~Roger

ROGER: It all started one harvest day. Mom and I worked in the potato house. Mom went in the house to cook supper. While she was getting supper, Herschel Smith called and told her that the carloads of potatoes that were shipped to Searsport for export were being kicked because of frost-damaged bags around the doors of the railroad cars. So, when everyone came in from the fields and potato house for supper, Mom told Dad about the railroad cars being kicked. Dad sent me out to get the International truck ready. I came back in and ate supper. After I was done we left for Searsport. I drove the truck down with one of the harvest workers, Larry Hede from New Sweden. Mom, my sister Barb, and Barney, another harvest worker and friend of the family, followed the truck in the Mercury Marquis. On the way I stopped at Flo's Inn and bought a case of Miller quickies. Larry and I drank a few driving south. I started driving the truck quite fast and reckless. A lot of it was the truck's fault. When I came onto a road crew working on the road in Houlton, I almost hit a car and knocked the safety cones into the path of oncoming traffic. Mom was extremely mad, trying to catch up to me and stop me. When I ran out of gas, she caught up to me. We had 15 gallons in cans with us. The whole time we were pouring gas in the truck, Mom was sassing me. She had Barney drive the truck to the gas station and then on to Searsport. When Barney got into the truck and seen all the empty beer bottles, he said, What did you have, two cases of beer?

I said, No, only one.

Mom sassed me at the gas station, at the motel in Searsport, and the next day, the next day, and the next day. I will probably get sassed again when she reads this. I didn't listen to sassing from Mom then, and I don't listen now.

Uncle Roland and Aunt Steffie came down the next morning with the pickup loaded with racks, conveyors, and equipment. We emptied the bad bags, re-racked, re-bagged, and reloaded the railroad cars, so they would pass inspection. As the railroad cars passed inspection, they would be loaded onto the ship. We not only reworked our cars but other growers' cars. We were there for a month or so. There was a restaurant and bar at the motel where we would have supper. That is where we met the captain of the ship, David Finn Dahl. The ship's name was *Nukualofa* [capital of Tonga Islands in the Southwest Pacific]. They were making several trips back and forth from Searsport to France until March, taking 30 days for each trip. We met him on his first trip. He told us we could work passage over and back. He also told us we would need passports. Uncle Roland was going to go, too. On November 2, we got all our shots and our passports finalized. On November 4, we went back to Searsport, and the ship left November 5, but Uncle Roland changed his mind. I had just graduated from high school, but I thought it would be a great opportunity to go over to France and see where the potatoes were going. Some of the potatoes on the ship were mine. I grew 20 acres of potatoes that year.

When we left Searsport it was at night and I was sleeping. We went in to Prince Edward Island to get fuel. That was where the ship ran aground and it put a big gash in the side of the ship. I did not know about this until we got to France. They ran the two forward bilge pumps the entire time going over to keep the ship afloat. If I had known about it I wouldn't have had such an enjoyable time. I don't think they told anybody except the people who needed to know.

The second day out to sea, my stomach was upset. They gave me a basket of fruit to eat to settle my stomach. It worked. I was not sick, just had a queasy stomach. The first and second day I ate with the captain and his officers and we got better or fancier meals. There were eight of us. After that I ate breakfast and supper with the captain and officers but had lunch with the crew. We had food breaks in between each meal. The food was good and plenty of it, even sweets, cakes, and cookies. The reason we were fed so well was that if we happened to go overboard, we could survive longer. They had this white meat in the chef salad that tasted like ham that I really liked. After a while I found out that it was raw fish. I still ate it because it tasted good. We would have whale steaks and shark meat. They caught a shark before docking.

When I was standing on the front ship—you know, like in the *Titanic* movie, where they're standing on the front of the ship—that's supposed to be the most spectacular part. There's a constant vibration with the engine propellers. I noticed it right away. When you first get on the ship, it's annoying, but then you get used to it. When the waves hit at the front it's got a thumping noise and you can feel that. The front moves up and down and bounces up and down. There's times when it feels like you're going to leave your feet if you hit a big wave right. You learn to walk funny.

I had the opportunity to stand up front and in the back. To me, you go in the back. It was quieter, and with the wake that's back there,

Potatoes being loaded aboard the Nukualofa

you would get to see the fish and gulls that swam around the wake. There was more activity in the back of the ship. It was smoother riding back there, nicer to stand back and watch than in the front of the ship. In the back you get the vibration of the engine and propeller, which is calmer, and you don't have that sudden jarring movement.

When we got to France, the captain told me about running aground in PEI while getting fuel and that they would have to go to dry dock in Belgium to get the ship repaired. It would take two to three months before we would get back to Searsport. He had me call home to let them know the situation.

At Searsport the railroad cars were unloaded and reloaded by longshoremen who slid them down a 50-foot wooden sluice and piled them on large palettes that were lifted with cranes and set down on the ship. Guys piled them around. Boards were laid across the bags in a haphazard manner and in different angles [dunnage] to keep the bags from moving. They weren't piled in tiers; they laid the bags flat. Every three layers they put a row of boards and alternated how the boards were laid on the potatoes. There were 500 to 550 110-pound bags per train carload. They handled them well here in the States, but when we got over there, they just threw them around like bags of cement. They busted them all up. In France they were having a severe famine and people were scavenging and saying how good the potatoes were. They were taken over there to be used for seed. Anything that was left laying around was scavenged. The potato crop was only about 15 percent for three years in a row.

It took seven days to unload the potatoes in France. The docks were in a levy and there were over 200 ships like the one I was on. Ships could only go in on high tide. They were all loading and unloading. The train cars were antique and smaller than what we use here, even in Aroostook County.

Not in France, but especially in Belgium, they were hoping that their daughters would meet somebody and get married to somebody from a wealthier country. Germany was the same way. Just being an American gave me a bonus. I was more of a target. In Belgium and Germany they would make food for you and bring it to you like a picnic, to the one they were interested in, sit down, and give you a meal. I was young and naive, I guess, but it's one of the most interesting experiences in my life. It sticks with me the most. In France it took two hours to get cleared to leave the ship. I was able to get right into the city to sailors' bars, not like a regular bar in the States. In the sailors' bars, there were lots of people to talk with, play checkers, darts, pool and drink warm beer with. Almost everyone spoke English there. Outside of those places, it was hard to find someone who spoke English.

After unloading in France we went through the English Channel, and down the Rhine River to Germany, to pick up steel. Just going over and right back, then watching them unload the potatoes—that was exciting—but to go down the Rhine River was so enjoyable. The beauty of the Rhine River is just unbelievable. That's got to be one of the prettiest places in the world—beautiful scenery, grass, trees, and castles. I've traveled around the United States. The Grand Canyon area I could compare to it, other than the fact that there's no green. It is spectacular like that. I would recommend it to anyone. It was more exciting than my trip to the Pyramids in Egypt. When I was in school, we had a teacher, Merle Smith, who said that one from that whole school might get to go over to the Pyramids, and I happened to be the one.

The people in Germany would speak English while working with you loading the boat, but when done work, they did not understand English. Trying to find a place to eat or asking how far away Hahn Air Force Base was, no one could understand what I was saying. Aunt Loretta and Paul were stationed in Germany then. When I told the captain about this, he said that is the way the Germans are. They do not like Merchant Marines and they did not want them to socialize with their families. We were in Germany for two days. Went in at night and left at night.

On the way to Antwerp, Belgium, where we unloaded two-thirds of the rolled steel, we met an Exxon supertanker carrying crude oil. It was on its way to a Scandinavian country. It was the largest ship in the ocean and made our ship look like a canoe. The Belgium docks are the largest in Europe and there were thousands of ships. It is also the largest dry dock in the world for repairing ships.

We weren't supposed to go to Germany. We were supposed to bring back just nails. Because they couldn't get right into dry dock, we went up to Germany and picked up steel to cover time until we could get in for repairs and brought it back to Antwerp, Belgium. It's so amazing to see how they brought the ship into dry dock, set it down on the timbers. They set up for repair. When they were working on it, you could walk through the hole in the ship. It was a pretty good-sized hole to be going across the Atlantic with 120 train carloads of potatoes. I don't know much the ship weighed, but it was pretty good weight, I'm sure, and there were 28 people on it and they just went across like it's no big deal.

We went to dry dock there. They flood the dock, open the gates and winch the ships in. Ten or twelve scuba divers go underwater to tie the ship and then it is winched on shore, the water pumped out of the ship, and then set on massive timbers, one foot by one foot, and 20 to 30 feet long. The sheets of steel to repair the hole were 20 feet by 12 feet, and one and a half to one and three-quarter inches thick. It took three sheets to repair the hole. They also replaced the bearings and shaft on the propeller.

While in Antwerp I walked through the city. Nice buildings and all manicured lawns. One building stood out from the rest. I found out that it was the Gold Trade. In Belgium there were brothel houses up and down the street—women sitting in windows, inviting you in. The streets had a bus stop building and outhouses with no doors. Everyone used them—men and women. The automobiles were antique-looking, small, with one person and three wheels. I bought Mom a clock there for a Christmas present. The clock had a light and a windmill.

We were in dry dock until 6:30 p.m. December 24th. Then, we left Belgium Christmas Eve during a most beautiful sunset, like the ones you see on the Pacific Ocean. I was standing, looking over the bridge of the ship. The captain asked me if it bothered me, being away from home for Christmas. I said, No.

Thirteen *is* a Lucky Number

It was my first Christmas with no white, and it was my first true-blue Christmas: perfectly blue skies, clear blue water, and my first Christmas away from home. When we left Belgium, everything was blue. Seen icebreaker ships, but no icebergs.

While in Antwerp, we loaded the rest of the ship with board nails. We stayed along the European coast until we were 100 miles off the coast of Spain before crossing the ocean for home. We went below the Bermuda Triangle to avoid heavy storms before heading north. Coming back, we were celebrating New Year's when the second mate came down at 10:30 p.m. to say we were coming into rough seas. By 1:00 a.m. we were in 30-foot waves. It was two to three days of rough seas. Schools of blue swordfish, five to six feet long, would be jumping in the waves and land on deck. We filled four or five 55-gallon drums. We took them below, cleaned them and put them in the freezer. Half of the crew were Tongans, and they would eat the fish as we cleaned it—raw. The captain and officers were Norwegian. The radio operator was Indonesian and was wanted for murders in Indonesia. The captain had told me not to be alone with him. After the seas calmed down we saw four whales. They were off in the distance but they were big. We went near the bottom of the Bermuda Triangle and nothing strange happened. We did not disappear.

The crew did not watch TV. The whole time I was gone, I did not watch any TV or listen to the radio. No Walter Cronkite, Donny and Marie, or Lawrence Welk (didn't miss him).

We stopped in North Carolina for five days to unload the steel and half of the nails. I went through U.S. customs four times, but I wasn't allowed off the ship because they were checking out why an American was on a Norwegian ship with a Tongan crew. It didn't seem right. Same thing in Philadelphia. We were in Philadelphia for six days to finish unloading. On the seventh day at 4:00 p.m. they said I could get off the ship, but we were leaving at 8:00 p.m. so I

Roger coming home

was not able to see the Liberty Bell. From where we were docked you could see the roof of the building that has the Liberty Bell in it. I just wanted to go see that.

After that, we went up into the New York Harbor and we went by the Statue of Liberty. That kind of appeased me because that was just amazing to see it coming in that way. For one thing, I never really expected to ever see something like that, because I was prepared to live on the farm all my life. That trip was just out of the blue. While the pilot was on the ship, they let me steer the ship while going through the New York area, by the Statue of Liberty, and under the George Washington Bridge. It was really something going by the Statue of Liberty. Impressive. All I could think of was the stories for- eigners told when they saw the Statue of Liberty. I felt the same way when we were in New York Harbor. Customs came with a boat and let half the crew go off ship for four hours. Then they came and got the other half. I wasn't allowed off because I was a U.S. citizen and I hadn't cleared customs. They didn't even try to clear me. They just told me I wasn't getting off the ship. Once cleared, customs rules everywhere would not allow me to go more than two miles from ship.

We stayed in Hudson Bay for two days waiting for the weather to clear. Then we went to Searsport and sat in the harbor six days. On the third day they came and told me I was cleared and I could go home.

When I got home I found out that customs had contacted the school, the Presque Isle Police Department, and the State Police Department to see if I had done anything or if there was anything to do with drugs. There was no reason for someone my age to be on that ship with all foreigners. Very unusual. They were suspicious. I didn't get that. In Germany they made me go to the captain's quarters. You file through one at a time. When I got there they made me talk to them right away because they had seen the American passport. One guy actually left with my passport because we were in dock. He came back an hour and a half later and said I was okay to get off the ship.

There was nothing in France as far as I know. I had no idea because we turned our passports in to the captain and he come back and gave it to me two hours later. I was able to get right into the city to sailors' bars. In Belgium, I was the only one that customs asked to see. They asked why I was on the boat. I explained that I farmed, that they were shipping potatoes to France. I had the opportunity to go and I went. They okayed it right there, signed papers, and said I was free to go off. I had to carry the papers with me. I'm glad that it happened that way.

Then I came back to Aroostook County. I left on November 5, 1976 and returned February 6, 1977. I was supposed to be gone only 30 days. I was gone three months.

Trucking

I'm a professional bum. I don't do anything I don't want to do. I used to farm. I got done farming and went into driving truck. I was supposed to get a job in Michigan working for Seneca Foods. When I went out there in October 1998, the man I had been talking to had a stroke and there was someone else in charge who wasn't going to have me start until May. So, to pass the time, I decided to try driving truck on my own and see some of the Unites States. I enjoyed it, so come April I called Seneca and told them to look for someone else. I could make as much money by myself with the truck. I don't have to deal with any hassles, just traffic, and that's different every day. I bought my own truck in 2002, a Freightliner Century Class. I'm leased onto Landstar. I look on the computer at the list of jobs available. I choose the one I want and call the broker. I work about seven months of the year. I take the rest of the year off. After April and I got married, she went with me on the road for six months. She decided it wasn't the lifestyle for her. She didn't like the fact that she wasn't making her own money, and traffic really bothered her. She'd be in the passenger seat. In two lanes of traffic you can't move over and you do have the right of way, but you can't stop for every car coming off the ramp, and they'll challenge you to see if you're going to slow down for them. She couldn't stand that, or the truck stops. April works for Clarke County in Berryville, Virginia.

I don't like the heat in Virginia but don't like the cold anymore either. You can run an air conditioner easier than you can run a woodstove. It's just a switch with an AC. I always heated with wood in Maine.

Growing up on a farm helps with things that come up suddenly. Some people get shocked that it's a major thing. Being with a large family and raised on a farm, that was just a normal, everyday thing.

Thirteen *is* a Lucky Number

There was always somebody getting hurt, always somebody having trouble with school, trouble with a friendship. Fifteen people: you tell me a day when there wasn't something happening. It prepares you but it teaches you not to be melodramatic. No soap opera in our lives, just that people lived it when we were young, and that was it. Everyday life now.

When I was the driver rep at MS Carriers [Family Dollar Account], I got to meet every driver who was on the account. We had one driver who would work three months and take a month off to go home. His family was in Syria. He was an American citizen and he had his three boys go over to Syria to get an education in the religion.

One day at breakfast, where drivers would meet to tell me their complaints, Mohammed asked five of us if we wanted to go to Syria with him. A couple weeks later, I had just come back from home and the fishing trip and I said, Well, things happen for a reason. I may never get another chance to go over there, so I went. It cost me my plane ticket over and I was there for three weeks. While I was over there, as part of their family's customs, they refused for me to buy anything, even souvenirs. If somebody visits them, they take care of them. His family and two aunts and uncles, a couple of their children's families, his family, and I traveled all around Syria, the Mediterranean Sea, and Turkey by bus. We saw a lot. I came back after three weeks but he stayed the whole month.

I got back on August 30, 2001. He was supposed to get back on September 11th. They turned his plane around two hours [11:30 a.m.] before it was supposed to land at Dulles Airport because the planes had hit the buildings in New York. They went back to Spain. All international traffic was stopped for three days. My friend didn't get back until October 16th. I had no idea that his plane got rerouted. I knew he was supposed to land that day and I called him on the cell phone three or four times. Another friend kept calling, too. That friend asked me if it

April and Roger, 2003

seemed like someone was listening when you called Mohammed. Yes, there are all kinds of funny clicking noises on the phone.

157

Mohammed called when he got into D.C. and said he would be at the storage lockers and we'd go have lunch. I got there 15 minutes after the time that he said he'd be there. We had rental lockers where we stored extra stuff. About ten minutes later a guy from the FBI came in and interviewed both of us. He asked Mohammed a lot more questions than anybody, but why was I over there? What was the purpose? But who am I? I'm not smart enough to be anybody. They knew about my passport and plane ticket. They admitted that they were tracking all cell phone calls. That was the clicking noises on the phone. That kept up for almost six months. When you said certain words— terrorist, terrorist attack—those would make an instant click come on. We'd sit around with the speakerphone on and joke and talk. Other people would know that the FBI was actually monitoring us. Even in conversation, discussing the news, like, I see they caught another terrorist, you'd hear that click. I would rather know that they were checking this. Intruding on my privacy? I wish they had intruded on a few more people's privacy. There might be less people dead.

Mohammed bought his own truck about the same time I did. He crosses the border a lot with the company he works for. They check him constantly, more because of his nationality and name than his looks. He goes by his nickname, Mo. He rarely says Mohammed to anybody because it's so much extra hassle. He's Mr. Average Joe, one of the nicest guys you'd ever want to meet, does everything he can for his family. He wouldn't do anything bad against anybody.

Canoe Trips

It started because nobody would go hunting and fishing with me. My brothers, brothers-in-law, and friends didn't have any interest in hunting and fishing. I used to go with my ex-father-in-law, and

Arnold Haines, people who were older than me. I always enjoyed it.
Did some of that with my grandfather. None of the kids were doing
that—Jason or Brent—none of them. They seemed interested in
going with me if I went bird hunting on the farm or fishing in the
farm pond. I started the fishing trips with a few of the nephews.
There were three the first year, eight the second year, and then it
went up into the twenties. The third year, my brother Mike went
along. I think there were 21 of us. We went for six or seven years in
a row. It just got to be too much. That last year there were 57 people
that came to the rented camp over the three days. It's too much to
plan, way out of hand, since I'm not up there anymore. I used to do
the cooking. We had fun. They are highlights.

I planned the fourth year, the trip that we came down the river,
and there was a drought. The weekend before we were supposed to
go on Saturday afternoon, it started raining and it rained right
through until Monday, and we got two and a half inches of rain. The

b: Jason, Dave, Gary, Jim, Mike, Sean, Stuart
m: Dan, Thomas, Brad, Anthony, Alan
f: Ethan, Roger

Aroostook River was at flood levels. When we come down, we didn't even have to paddle or anything. There's a little old dam up in Ashland. We went over that and it was just a ripple. Normally you'd have to get off and go around.

Near the end of the trip it was threatening rain again, so we went and stayed in one of the potato houses that I owned. The kids slept in the stacked wooden potato ventilators that weren't being used. [Ventilators are 16 feet long and 2-by-8-foot structures, built of wooden slats, with fans on both ends to ventilate the potatoes stored in the potato house.] They played that they were caskets. We built a fire in there and it rained all that night. Sean and Stuart slept together on a palette. When they got up in the morning they chased each other around. Sean said, I didn't leave Stuart alone all night. Well, Stuart spoke up without thinking. Yeah, I had to beat him off all night long.

Things like that happened. We had a food fight. Canoe trips for three years with just kids, never once had a food fight. I don't think we lost but one plate of spilled meat. Take the adults along and we had a food fight. Three or four loaves of bread, couple dozen eggs.

Little House

We fooled around at night and Dad would come to sass us. The ceiling was only about five-foot-eight and being over six foot, he'd always bump his head. It used to create laughter. Then he'd spank one and another one would start tee-heeing and giggling. He'd stand up again and hit his head again. I don't know how often that actually happened but it seemed like it was on a regular basis. We weren't the best kids! There was a little bit of mischief in all of us. I think we had respect for people, but I think we also liked to have fun.

My Grandparents

I have a lot of special memories of my Grampy Campbell. We were born on the same day. Depending upon who you talk to, I was the worst or best birthday present that Mom could have ever given him. I was about nine years old before he finally let me have a birthday. He used to make me cry every year on my birthday. It was our birthday and I'd be all excited. Nope, it's *my* birthday, he'd say. You can't have one. It was just teasing.

He bought me a pony for my fifth birthday. He bought it from the people at the fair. It had been at the fair for nine or ten years. All its life it had been a fair pony, walking around the loop for kids to have a ride. It was a very large Welsh pony. After we got it, for three or four days, all it would do is go around this lilac bush. On the third day I told Grampy, Well, jeez, can't this horse do anything better? I want to do like on TV. I want to go ride down around the fields.

He said, Well, I'll get it to go.

He cut a branch off the lilac tree and slapped it on the butt. There was an apple tree just beyond that, going up toward the Gilmans'. There was a branch just high enough for the horse to go under, but it caught me right in the stomach and took me right off. His name was Flicka, after the show, *My Friend Flicka*. We used to watch that show. His name before Flicka? I have no idea. I guess his name used to be number 21. We're picking the mind and memory of a five-year-old here.

My grandfather treated me very well. The only graduation he went to was mine. I always had an extra special feeling for Grampy Campbell. Looking back, he treated me much better than any of the other kids. I can remember Mom coming down and sassing Grampy Campbell a couple different times because, when I was four years old, he put me on the tractor to drive through while he picked rocks. It was a Farmall Regular and I would steer it. It had a regular clutch and hand brakes and when we'd come to the end of the row, he would jump on the draw bar; or when somebody called, Whoa, either him or Dad would jump on and stop it. I never turned on the ends. I held it going down through the rows. That's how I learned to drive a tractor. I was just a little better than a rock. If they'd had bungee cords, I could have been replaced with a bungee cord.

Grampy would take me bird hunting out around the farm. I'd ride around with Grampy all the time, so I don't know if he took me to go bird hunting or he just happened to be bird hunting and I went.

My grandfather and Uncle Tom were monster men—both six-foot-two or six-three, 300 pounds. They were overweight, but not fat overweight. Grammy was about six-foot-one. I was 14 by the time I got to be as tall as she was. She was the same height as Dad. I can remember that. Right after that, she began shrinking because of her age. She was proud of herself and she always stood straight. I think of her when I'm driving truck because you kind of need to slouch. Truck drivers probably have the poorest posture of anybody because you're sitting hours on end. There's nothing to do. You develop poor posture. Every once in a while, I think of Grammy and I think, boy, she would flick me with her fingers behind the ears, or she would slap my knee and tell me to sit up straight. She'd preach, You're going to have slouching shoulders. When I think of Grammy, I sit up straight and watch my posture because I don't want slouching shoulders.

She made molasses donuts and fresh bread. You could go up there and she'd tell you not to take it but you could take one. You know she seen you do it, but if you went and tried to take two, you got in trouble. You weren't supposed to take any but could always sneak one.

Both Grammy and Grampy lived through the Depression. They both had hard times. I don't know what their finances ever were, but I always felt that they could have lived a better life, traveled more; they could have had nicer things. But everything that they had they had high respect for, they treated it real well, and they got by with very little. They seemed like the kind of people who chose to live the way they did.

I have a lot of good feelings for both of my grandparents. My Grammie and Grampie Guerrette, too. I'm glad I knew them. They were good people to know. Grampy Campbell was always kind of *grrrahrah*. Kind of grumpy and stern. With Grampie Guerrette, it was . . . okay. If you did something wrong, he had a way of dealing with it. He was the type of person that you just respected the way he was and you did what he wanted. The same thing with Grampy Campbell. He was grumpy and growly, but if you did what he wanted, he never said anything to you. He was just Grampy.

When we were at Grampie and Grammie Guerrette's camp, we used to get sassed for walking halfway across the lake. We'd walk out to where it'd be up to our shoulders and you could walk across. It's terrible. It's called Mud Lake for a reason. My grandfather used to haul in shale; 15 or 20 dump-truck loads were dumped in the lake, so there was a base and you didn't have to walk in so much mud. You get beyond the shale and you'd be up over your ankles in mud. Gross. Bloodsuckers, dragonflies. A big pile of mud! We had a lot of fun there.

About the time I got to high school, when everyone went up for a week, I stayed home. I had other things going of more interest. I did the spraying, which took more than three days. I rode a motorcycle and tented out back. Dad went up and back every night.

Harvest

In the fall of the year we all had to work on the harvesters and in the potato houses. Those who weren't good workers had to go in and get the meals ready. Barb [15 or 16 years old] and Jim [10 or 11 years old] were some of the not-good workers, and they got stuck with the cooking. Besides me, we all had to take turns. I think I was more valuable out working than I was in cooking. Barb went in to cook. Mom used to tell them what had to be cooked. Barb made a roast, boiled potatoes, corn on the cob, green salad, and cabbage. The only thing wrong with Barb, she doesn't know the difference between lettuce and cabbage. She boiled the lettuce until there was no more water, causing it to burn. I still tease Barb about burning the lettuce when she went in to make supper. Poor Jim, smart guy, but just doesn't have it all up there. He went in one time and decided that instead of just regular old potatoes, he wanted french fries. He peeled up all of the potatoes, cut them all in the french-fry shape and, like for our family, we had a two-gallon bucket that we cooked potatoes in. He put them in the water and boiled them on the stove and they turned to mush. He didn't know that you had to cook them in grease. He makes the mushiest french fries you ever had. That fall, those were my two memorable meals. And Mom, to tell you the type of person she is, both times she come in, never sassed either one of them. We all teased the crap out of them. She just said, That's all right, and she went about and made something else to take its place. And that was it. Mom used to laugh when we teased them but she never put in. I'm sure she'd like to. I'm sure there are things that I did that she could have teased about, too. Now, the others are so good-hearted, they won't tell the truth. I tease Mom. She hates it. Things like that I don't let people forget because that's all part of life. That's one of the good things.

Telling on Sherrill

There was a big outing. I had two snowmobiles at the time, so Jason, Brent, Danny, and Brad went. Barb, Stuart, Janelle, Dave, Sherrill, a couple others, and myself all went up through Caribou, Van Buren, and over to the Lakeview Restaurant in St. Agatha to have lunch and back down. Dave and Sherrill's sled was a small one-up sled and the two of them was riding on it, so on the way up, I kept offering them one of my sleds with the two-up seat, and they wouldn't use it. Just stayed running on that little sled. By the time we got to the Lakeview, everybody was pretty much starved to death because it took an hour and a half longer than what we had anticipated on getting up there. We went in to eat and it made Sherrill have an upset stomach because she had gone so long without eating. We went to leave to come back and, instead of riding on the back, she started driving. She'd only drive 25 to 30 miles an hour. We kept having to stop for her. We come to one place where we stopped. You come off the lake and there's a big, steep snowbank you have to go down, and you're onto a flat part where everybody stops and parks. Here comes Dave and Sherrill. We've been waiting about five minutes for her. Sherrill's driving. You could see her. Then all of a sudden the sled disappears because it had to go down in this little gulley and up over this bank. And you can hear, she never lets off the sled, so she goes over this bank. She should be going only five or ten miles an hour over and she comes up over it 25 to 30 miles an hour, jumps into the middle of the road, lands right in the middle of the road. Her and Dave almost bounce off. She gets it stopped and under control, shuts it off and she says, Well, what are you waiting for? (Like that was how you were supposed to come in.)

It was so funny. She comes down there, didn't realize it was there, jumped, plop, and boom. Then, she says, Well, let's go, I'm ready.

Sherrill keeps telling me that she's the favorite sister-in-law.

Sisters

One time Nason McGlinn made a comment to me about my sister Sharon. He said, She's an angel on earth. It was when they were building the garage where Sharon's family lives. She's working at MFX and taking care of her kids. She was having a barbecue that weekend. He has a lot of respect for Sharon for all she does. She's always smiling and happy.

Sharon's a lot like Mom. Mom works and works. She took care of all of us. What did she ever get for thanks? The only thanks I think Mom gets is at Christmas dinner, when everybody shows up, she gets to cook for everybody again. She gets to see everybody talking and telling stories. That seems to be the only thanks that Mom gets. Mom never says much. I think she feels fortunate for the good things she's got and she doesn't let the bad things bother her.

Roger at Kim and Kevin's wedding luau

I helped Kim when she was going to move back up to Maine from Atlanta, Georgia. Because she was a flight attendant, she had two places. We went first to Atlanta, on to Cincinnati, and then to Maine. One of the comments after the trip that she put in the thank-you note that she sent me was that she never knew me. Some of the stories she'd heard about me, she didn't know if she really wanted to ask me about because she thought I'd be grouchy and grumpy. And that always struck me as the difference in the age. She'd never seen me grow up. By the time she knew me, I was working on the farm all the time, or off working.

By the way, when Dad came down to the campground to scare us kids in the tent, I just pretended I was scared to make them think I was scared.

CHAPTER FOURTEEN

Growing Up

You couldn't even run away from home. There were so many of us; they wouldn't even miss you.
    ~Barb

BARB: I was always trying to keep up with my brothers. I definitely was a tomboy. Sharon and Pat, the older sisters, were always sewing or cooking or doing something inside, and yuk, yuk. So, I always tried to be with the guys. Mom was going to take one of the pigs to be slaughtered. Well, the boys always got to go and I thought, why can't I go? So, she never wanted me to go but she let me go this time. We're going down the road to the slaughterhouse, which was in Mars Hill. All of a sudden, the box that the pig was in falls off and the pig got out. We were near Roger's Market. I don't remember how we got the pig back in the box but we did. We get to the slaughterhouse and it seemed like I wasn't out of the pickup very long and the guy comes out with a gun and shoots the pig right between the eyes. Oh, my goodness, what a shock! Down goes the pig. They pull the pig out of the truck and into the slaughterhouse and they slice it down the center and pull it apart, or put it on this thing and take the skin off it. It's like, oh, that's all I could see. I never wanted to go see a pig be slaughtered again. The guys made it sound like it was fun. Maybe it was for them. Mom didn't watch it, she just drove. Just the smell in the place, too, was something you'd never lose.

The other thing was animals. I was looking for Mom one day. I think she had a phone call or something and someone said she was in the shop, which was like a little machine shop where tools were. So, I open up the little side door and we seldom went into that room in the barn. There's my mother, Amy McGlinn, Beth Morris, Nason McGlinn. Nason's cutting the chickens' heads off and all the girls have on these rubber gloves and they're pulling the feathers off. I quit eating chicken.

My brother Dave and I had little things that we got into. Little events. We were very mischievous. We were very close in age and I guess we thought alike. We lived in what we called the little house until 1968, when Kim was born, and my grandparents lived in the bigger house up on the hill. I can't believe so many of us lived in that little house. Oh, my goodness, when you're a little kid, everything seems big, and you don't think of that stuff, but when my Uncle Roland and Aunt Steffie lived there and I went down there, I thought, how did we all fit in this house? I remember all these cribs in one room and Mom and Dad's bed. We had to pull this ladder down to get upstairs. It was kind of neat. Those were our unique times! Upstairs was all one room with your slanted ceilings. The girls' side, we painted it pink, and the boys' side was blue. We'd go up the ladder and get in our beds and there were all these twin beds all over the place. And, of course, with so many of us, there were three girls on one side and three boys on the other. We'd have to go to bed at a certain time and we'd get to talking and laughing and Dad would come up and say, Hey! You guys go to sleep!

Well, he had to duck his head and he'd bump his head and we'd start laughing. Then he'd say, Hey! I don't want to hear your laughing. No laughing.

We'd try not to laugh and you could tell he's trying not to laugh, too. He'd go back downstairs. That was fun. There were these little cubbyholes where the ceiling slanted down. We always had to take naps in the afternoon before we started school, even when we were in school. During vacations we'd still take these naps and I hated to sleep, so I'd usually lay there with my eyes open, thinking all these things I could be doing. Well, Dave wasn't sleeping either this one day. We opened up this cubby and we see this candy and started eating it. It was real pretty, like a bride and groom, I think. Mom had saved some of their wedding cake and we were eating it.

These times we had to take naps—one time we opened the window. Didn't wake up the other kids. We climbed down the fire-escape ladder. Dave was probably down three steps and I was out the window. All of a sudden, we heard Mom: Hey, what are you guys doing? She had a laundry basket with her. We both turned around and we jumped off that ladder. Oh, I swear to God, my legs went right into my back. I couldn't believe I jumped. We had to go back upstairs and take our naps. Mom said we couldn't get away with anything and we got caught quite a bit. The Campbell kids could never get away with anything anywhere. One reason is because we looked alike.

Another time we were taking our naps; I must have gone to sleep that time, but next thing I heard noise downstairs. I went downstairs and Dave had his fingers in a big silver bowl. I looked in and it was all red inside and I wondered what happened. He had gone up to the potato house and they were racking potatoes. He got his finger stuck in the rack. I don't know if he was supposed to be out there or not. But in my mind, every time something would happen, Mom would say, God punished you and I'm thinking, ohhhh, he didn't take his nap. God punished him because he cut the top of his finger off.

Other things that we did: We'd go up to my grandmother's. There was a porch. At the time it didn't have any windows. It was all

open with a railing across. My grandfather had on one end shelves
with all his tools. There was a Sprite bottle up there. We were playing
doctor. Dave was the patient and I was pretending to take care of him
and I saw the Sprite bottle, so, I said, Okay, this will be your medicine
but don't really drink it. Just put it in your mouth and spit it out.

I swear to God that's what I said, but he must have drank it. I was
over at the tool cabinet and I could hear him going *ooahh, ooahh*. He
couldn't breathe and he kept doing that. I had to get my grandmother
and she was old. We didn't have a phone at the little house, and when
she saw Dave couldn't breathe she said, Go get your mother.

I actually think she brought my brother down to the little
house. Somehow he got down there. Mom asked, What did you do?

I had him drink some stuff [tarline, a solution that would
remove tar from cars] up there.

Mom mixed, I think it was milk and eggs, to try to make him
vomit. Then they took him to the hospital. I thought, I killed my
brother. That's all I could think—I killed my brother. I think they
pumped his stomach out and he was okay. It was scary. He always got
hurt. I never did.

BOB: Down in the little house we used to have a pot burner and a
five-gallon can of kerosene on it. It always leaked, so I put a dish under
to catch the drips. Barb and Dave got into that and Dave drank that.

During spring we used to dig dandelions and have fiddleheads
to eat. We had vinegar in a colored, striped glass jar on the table. We
were living in the old trailer then. Sharon was in the high chair. She'd
cry every day for that glass—Want that, want that—and she'd cry
and throw a fit, so I said one day, Do you want it?

She said, Yeah, so I gave it to her.

She just drank that right down. Ooooo. Couldn't get her to take
a drink for a month after that. She didn't cry anymore for that jar.

BARB: I think a lot about being on the farm. As one of the older kids, you think you could get away with things where the younger kids couldn't. Our parents were so busy with the younger ones. We were told to go outside and play and some of the things we did—if they only knew. They know this one thing, so I can tell this.

We were in the garage at the Ashby farm. It had a basement, like a lower level. We seldom went down there, but our neighbors Mark and Mike Gagnon had come up, and they had gotten cigars and we were going to smoke cigars. It was two of my brothers [also named] Mike and Dave, Mark and Mike, and me. First of all, we were trying to light the cigars and I think Mike was trying to do that. There must be a knack to it, because even though you have matches—you try to light it—that doesn't work. I remember Mike trying to take a big puff off it while lighting it, and that didn't work, so we talked about people cutting the ends off. So, we cut the end off and Mike took a big puff and got it lit. He got kind of nauseous so we passed the cigar around and each of us take a puff.

We start feeling dizzy and light-headed. So we thought, that's enough of that, but we were still in the basement and then somebody noticed a gas fuel tank. We wondered if there's any fuel in that, so we turned this little nozzle and this fuel or gas comes out, so we turned it off. Just throw a match on there and lit that little circle of fuel and it has this pretty rainbow light. We thought that was cool. We have a whole book of matches so we turned it on again and made a little bit bigger circle to see what that would look like, and we lit it. That was even prettier with prettier flames. We did it for quite a while. We got that thing really big. Why we didn't burn and why we didn't catch the place on fire, I don't know. I don't know why we stopped. Each of us had our turn to light it. Dave tattled to Mom, that's how she knows about it.

I was really upset one time and was going to run away from home. I left and went out behind the garage where there was a side hill. I just laid there. It seemed like I was there for hours. I came back home because nobody came out looking for me. I came back home and they didn't even know I was gone. You couldn't even run away from home. There were so many of us; they wouldn't even miss you.

Dave packed a bag and went down to that shed in the middle of the field at the Ashby place. He got scared and came back.

We were great big chickens. The front of the house had this big stone. We memorized it:

On the lawn at Ashby farm

Ashby farmhouse

ON THIS SPOT IN 1878
WILMONT T. AND ADA WARD ASHBY
BEGAN LIFE TOGETHER IN A LOG CABIN.
HERE THREE OF THEIR SIX CHILDREN
WERE BORN: FRANK, NELL AND FRED.
THIS MEMORY STONE PLACED BY
FRED D. ASHBY IN 1953.

We lived on a dirt road and there were these trees. It's kind of like the unknown of what's in those woods. So we played kick the can at night. The challenge was to run around the house. Well, if you ran around the house you had to go in that side where the stone was and it's real, real dark and there weren't any lights back there. I never was brave enough to run all the way around the house. I saw my brothers do it. I'd get so far and didn't dare and I'd turn around. For me it wasn't the stone, it was the woods. There was a huge maple tree that scared me. I was just a big chicken at night in the

175

dark. Also there was an old fertilizer storage shed one-quarter mile from our house. We were all afraid of that. We'd dare each other to go into that.

I couldn't wait to get my license and drive. So, I used to drive around the farm before I got my license and of course it was always standard [shift] vehicles. And the first time I drove I think I had to move a vehicle and Dad just said, You've got first, second, third and fourth gear. It's like, okay. I get in the vehicle and I go. I had moved vehicles several times or drove on field roads—field to field on the field roads. One day Dad was in the green International truck with me, maybe a year later. The way I always drove, I'd start in second gear because you're going faster and didn't have to shift as much because that was so hard to do, and then I went to fourth gear. He said, What are you doing?

I want to go faster so I'm shifting gears. Then he explained to me that you're supposed to go first, second, third, fourth. He might have told me that the first time but I only half hear things. So, I learned how to do that. I never really wanted to drive a standard after that.

My brother, Dave, he's a year younger than I am. We seemed to do a lot of things together. We seemed pretty close. I had my license at the time, so Dad asked us to take the garbage to the dump in Caribou. There are a lot of stop signs and I didn't do very good. I'd always stall when I'd try to get the vehicle going. So Dad said, Just press on the clutch and Dave will go with you and shift the gears.

So we go down the East Presque Isle Road and that was fine. We got to the stop sign but I could kind of roll through. There wasn't anything coming. We got on the bridge and I took a right, had to look a little bit and we were able to roll through there. We get into Caribou and I think there was a stop sign where the smoke shop is. I made it through that, but then we get to this other stop sign where I had to stop. There's a gas station on one side and a church on the other side. We stopped. There were a whole bunch of high school students in the churchyard. They were just standing there, seemed like a place they hung around, I guess. We started to go and I stalled and we went again and I stalled again. I stalled—I want to say five or six times. We finally get it going and the kids in that yard, they start clapping, Yay, she did it! The pickup has this *aaoogah* horn, so Dave's pressing *aaoogah*. I thought we were like the Waltons.

We do get out to the dump and we take care of the garbage. There was another friend that lived on Green Ridge with us, Clark Ewing, who followed us out there on a motorcycle. So, we were coming back on that road to come home. We were almost to the stop sign and we didn't see anything coming. I'll just shift it into fourth gear and we'll go right on the New Sweden road. We're going pretty fast. He shifts it but he puts it in second gear instead of fourth. We slow right down almost to a dead stop. We had to stop and got going again okay. We got home all right and Dad never knew until just recently. I took my driver's test three times. I drove on the farm but I didn't do well with stop signs. I avoid standard shift but I can drive a motorcycle.

The Fire

BARB: February 2, 1976. It was a winter night. Sharon and Terry were married and they had Jennifer. I had always begged Mom and Dad for a horse. Always. And one day, I'm not sure how that came about, but Ernest Chamberlain brought a horse over and said as long as I took care of it, I could have the horse. That February night before I went to Sharon and Terry's, I took care of the horse Toby, and went to babysit Jennifer. We got a call in the middle of the night, saying that the barn was on fire and that the house was on fire.

There was a wind and ice storm that froze. Nobody could drive or steer cars. The fire trucks couldn't get there. Everything was in the barn—snowmobiles that we had just bought from the base. I never even had a chance to ride those. There was a sad thing.

We lost the animals: the horse; Sun Van Della, our cow; chickens, except for one we called One Eye. The other chickens attacked it and it lost one and had the grossest growth on its eye. But we always kept it out of the chicken pen and that was Jim's chicken and she survived it. Some of the chickens that survived had no feathers and the neighbors took them. Sun Van Della was our registered 4-H Holstein cow from Mike Milbury's herd. We had three pigs. We always had pigs. These three pigs were the meanest pigs you've ever seen. They were dark red color. If you went to feed them you had to be so careful because they were just mean. It's kind of awful to say but I was glad they got burnt.

MARY: What's so bad about the fire was when I got there, the whole barn was pretty much gone. The next day you go and you see all the metal, but then to go and find out where the animals were. Did they try to go out? Roger tried to get the animals out but they wouldn't go. I remember reading in a book that you're supposed to put a blanket over their heads, but Roger said it didn't matter what you did, they wouldn't come out. That was our worst thing. To add to that, we lost all the farm equipment, and some potatoes.

———————

BARB: I loved being here in Fort Fairfield for my senior year. Where we lived on the farm, it was actually located in Presque Isle. Our mailing address was Caribou and our phone was Fort Fairfield. We went to Holy Rosary Convent School, grades one to six [it used to be one to eight], and we got on the Caribou school bus. We had three driveways to our house, like a horseshoe. When you got to seventh grade you went to Presque Isle and got on that bus. We'd always get teased that our family was so big we had to go to different towns. There was a line of kids for each bus. I think it was unique and I kind of liked that.

BOB: When we loaded potato trucks it took all day. They'd back it in. Sometimes the drivers would go to sleep in the truck because they had been driving. Most of them came in from Boston. Most of them would come in and have dinner with us. About quarter to four a bus would come and pull in. About five minutes later a bunch of kids all get off. A little later another would come, pull in and stop. The truck driver said, What do you fellers do, run a daycare center?

No, it's just the kids.

Jesus, all them kids? They're all yours? How come there's two buses?

He had the worst time over that.

Searsport Adventure

BOB: In the fall we shipped potatoes by rail to Searsport for loading on a ship. There was juice running out of some of the cars because the potatoes were spoiling on the cars before they were shipping. Well, because of that they started inspecting everybody's potatoes. They called me up and told me I had eight cars that were turned down. Well, I had killed [sprayed the vines with sodium arsenic and diesel fuel, instead of waiting for them to wilt] mine and I knew there was nothing wrong with them—that they weren't breaking down. What happened is the potatoes are in 110-pound bags and when they push them up into the car, the potatoes would bruise a little and make water spots on the bag. Any time they saw spots, they turned the whole car down. I said, There's no way, but I sent two trucks and sent five of you—Roger, Mary, Barney, Larry, and Barb. Sent them and all the equipment all the way down there to rack them over. This was going to cost us a lot of money. So, I said, You tell us what bag you want, we'll get the bag for you and you will inspect that. You say how many you want and we'll get them. And I'll guarantee there's nothing wrong with them.

We repacked only one car. Then we were the only ones there who could do that, so they hired us to do all these other cars. The cars that were turned down, they shipped back to us at home and had us re-grade them and sent them back down. This was during digging, too. It took us three or four months.

BARB: I learned how to chew my nails on that trip. It was neat to see all the different farmers there racking potatoes together. My Mom and I were the only women. The captain of the ship invited everybody to Jed's Restaurant in Belfast. It had a bar and nightclub area, too. Barney Barnett was one of our crew members. I was 16 years old. He said, Why don't we order you a drink. What are you going to have to drink?

I didn't know.

I'll order you a Shirley Temple.

I said, Can I have that?

He said, Sure, so it was this nice, pretty, red drink with a straw and I thought, this is so great. I think there was a cherry in it, too. So, I drank that and said, Wow, that's good, so he ordered me another one, and I thought I was really drinking alcohol. I must have had five of them and I didn't get really drunk. I thought, jeez, I can handle my liquor pretty well. Every time I got done drinking, Barney showed me how to put the glasses in my mother's big pocketbook so we'd have some nice glasses when we got home. They weren't plastic, they were glass. She found those that night.

The crew from the ship was there from all over. They didn't speak English. One liked me and asked me to dance. He kept saying something. I wasn't sure what he was saying, so the captain told me he was asking me to marry him. He gave me this gold bracelet that he might have made. Obviously, I didn't marry him.

How Stuart and I Met

BARB: I had gone to Canada one night with my sister Roberta, and her friend Sherry Finnemore. We hadn't gone out for quite a while, so we went to Friday's Club in Grand Falls, New Brunswick. We were sitting at this table in a corner. We had just ordered drinks and I had a beer. There were these three cowboys, like, sitting at the table next to us, and they were being really ignorant and making these strange remarks to us, so I thought, let's go move. Well, we saw a couple that we knew, good friends of ours, Jeff and Sherry Davenport. We thought we'd go sit with them. They had another couple with them. We knew the girl, but I didn't know the guy who happened to be Stuart. We go to move tables, so I finished filling my glass with the beer I had in my bottle. The glass was quite full. I forgot there were stairs, so I'm walking and there were these stairs. I start to fall and I went, Ooh. My arms went up in the air and there goes my beer all over the three cowboys in the corner. It went down my top. I had my favorite blue top on and it went all down the front of me, too. So, I go there and put my beer on the table. They kind of introduce me to Stuart and I said, Well, I got to fix myself up. So, I go to the ladies' room and come out and sit with them. Stuart and I got to talking. He didn't get up and dance with the girl he was with. We were sitting there for a while and finally Stuart wasn't dancing, so I asked him to dance and he danced with me a couple times. After that

Stuart and Janelle

we went home. I guess it was no big deal. He knew I spilt the beer all over me but I guess it wasn't that visible. But then after that I called him a couple of times and left a message to call me at my work. I guess he called at night and the phone would just ring and ring. He thought I was always out every night, so he didn't go out with a girl like me who was out all the time. Somehow we connected, I don't know how, but we started dating after that.

STUART: I'm not sure just what my impression of the Campbell family was. There are four boys in my family. The first time there was a big family gathering, I just set back and tried to take it all in. It was the Christmas of 1986 and there was a big storm. Everybody stayed here except me. I lived close by. It came time to leave. I gave her a kiss before I left and embarrassed her. Doreen was out in the kitchen. She didn't want to be kissed in front of anyone.

BARB: I never wanted to fall in love.

STUART: She didn't want me around, but I was too numb to catch on. She'd do whatever she could to drive me away, but for some reason, somehow, I hung on.

BARB: Stuart is from Fort Fairfield but I didn't know him. He was shy. Wicked shy. It's hard to tell but he's younger than I am. I'm kidding.

STUART: After the night we met, I stayed away from her because I thought she was still in high school. I just got home from the service. I rarely went out and this was one of the few nights I went out, and I didn't want to get tangled up with anyone who was still in high school. I used to work at Northeast Publishing, printing the newspapers and I worked weird hours. I was home one Wednesday afternoon and the phone rang and I answered it. It was her and she thought she was calling her brother Mike. She was all confused. I told her it was Stuart and we started talking.

BOB: New ones coming into the family have to be pretty strong. He takes a lot of ribbing and teasing.

MARY: But he fit right in too well.

STUART: I always made up for it, though. I gave it right back.

Stuart, Barb, Jason and Janelle

Dave's 30th birthday was coming up. Sherrill called me one day and she wanted to throw him a surprise party. But she wanted me to get him out of the house so everyone could get there and get things set up. I said, Sure. It was in the wintertime and I was coming over to Fort to pick up snow sleds so Jason could drive one instead of riding double. I asked Dave and he said he'd love to go, so I picked him up. Sherrill told me to have him back by seven.

We went to my parents' house, picked up the sled, and when we got back it was still early. Barb was working at The Jade as a cocktail waitress. We stopped into the bar, set down and ordered a drink. Barb brought us a drink first. When people found out it was Dave's birthday, everyone started buying us drinks. I started looking at my watch, thinking it was time to go, but how do I do it without letting him know it was a surprise party? We had two or three beers on the table. We didn't know it, but there was a storm going on. We

b: *Jacob, Barbara (holding Madison and Emily), and Jonathan*
f: *Noah, Nicole, Kayla*

184

got to feeling pretty good. There were some girls in tight pants. I told Dave, Look over your left shoulder.

Well, it was his right shoulder. He looked the wrong way. No, no, your other left shoulder. Well, time went on. We didn't know it but the power went out on the far side of town where the party was. Sherrill was setting there and the longer it took for us to get there, the madder she got. The power went off at The Jade, too. The emergency lights went on, but the phone wouldn't work, so even though Sherrill called, the phone rang, but not in the building.

BARB: Meanwhile, everyone was setting down to Sherrill's waiting for us to show up at nine o'clock. I kept saying to Stuart, You got to get him home.

We got all these beers—I can't, Stuart said.

Mary was down to Sherrill's. Terry volunteered to go get Dave. She told him to set right down and stay right here. Terry got mad because he had to stay with all the women there and he's pretty sure we're out drinking. Sherrill's family started leaving. About 9:15, I finally got him there. We didn't even get out of the pickup. Sherrill met us with a flashlight. Where the hell have you been?

So, I still take a ribbing for that.

MARY: Stuart was no longer her best neighbor.

STUART: No, I was on the outs for a while, but Dave says to this day that's the best birthday party he ever had.

BARB: When the lights went out, it got even better.

Canoe Trip

STUART: Roger had a tradition of taking all the nephews on a fishing trip. We did it every year for several years. This one year he decided he'd take all the brothers-in-law and nephews. We put in at Ashland for

Janelle, Barb and Jason, 1999

a two- or three-day trip. The teasing started way before we got up there. We had seven canoes and 17 or 18 of us. We planned to float all the way to Roger's farm in Caribou. On the way up we stopped in at Sears to pick up some propane cylinders. There was a hurricane in Florida and talk of it coming up this way. The weather was going to get bad. At Sears the woman asked us, Aren't you worried? That hurricane's on the way up. You guys could get caught out there.

We told her with what we put up with at home with the women, that a little bit of wind ain't going to bother us none. She didn't like that but Roger thought it was pretty good. We walked out of the store and Roger was still laughing. We got to Ashland, put in and started floating down through. We did okay the first day. Brad, brother Jim and his son Ethan rode with Roger. Part of the deal to get Jim to go: Roger told him that he didn't have to do anything. He could just go along with the ride. Jim said, Fine.

Roger had canoe buddies. You tie two canoes together side by side and lock them together. We barely started and we came to an old dam to float over. The water was fairly high, and right at that point, it was kind of tough, so Roger asked Jim to help him. They were going sideways, so it was going to be dangerous when they come over. Roger said, Jim, grab a paddle there and help me get this straightened out.

Jim just looked at Roger and said, Nope; you told me if I came along I didn't have to do anything and I'm not doing anything. I'm going to just set here and enjoy the ride.

Somehow Roger got it turned and they got over it fine. But when they got on the other side, they weren't long switching canoe buddies. We camped along the Aroostook River that night.

Next day the weather was starting to get bad, so we thought we'd make some extra time. We floated as far as Washburn and met up with Terry and Sharon and had lunch. Terry decided to come with us from there down. He thought he could make it to the potato house, no problem. So we got going along and he told Roger, Boy, this would be a lot more fun if you'd brought a motor. You wouldn't have to paddle.

We let him talk about it for a couple hours. Finally said, Terry, look behind you.

He turned and looked and the motor was setting behind him. He wasn't too impressed. He called us a few names.

Once the weather starting getting bad enough, we decided we better make some time, so we tied all seven canoes together, all the way across, with the canoe buddies we'd had and with ropes. We had two motors, so we hooked the motors and we started making time.

We got clear to Presque Isle. We unhooked them and everyone went their separate way again.

We got just on the other side of Presque Isle and a big water fight broke out. We had seven canoes and everyone had pots and pans, empty two-liter soda bottles. We filled them all up and soaked everyone. In one canoe were Dave, myself, Dave's boys, Danny, and Brad. We looked around. We had no pots or pans, no soda bottles. All we had was half a paddle and all we could do was splash people. We were getting wet, bad. We happened to look and we had a cooler setting there. Opened up the cooler and there was 13 dozen eggs.

Boys, we're going to get even.

So I threw one egg at Roger. It skipped across the water and went between his life vest and stayed right there. Didn't break. He took it out, threw it back and it went in our canoe and didn't break. I picked it up. Are these damned things hard-boiled?

Yeah, so I took it right into the side of my head and egg run down.

Roger was fighting a migraine headache up to then and when I threw the egg he got mad. But as soon as I broke it into the side of my head, that broke the stress. We were almost at the potato house, four miles. Just like McHale's Navy out there on the river. Everyone started paddling their canoes around. The ones who had motors were circling and throwing water and all of a sudden, the eggs and wet bread started flying. We must have emptied six dozen eggs.

I can't swim. We were putting the boats in. Got everything unloaded all except one boat. They hollered for me to go way to the back and take up the back of the boat so we could pull it out. I didn't think nothing of it. Sure, we'll get it out. I got beyond halfway to the boat and three people piled right on top of me. Pay back for the eggs and all the wet bread and splashing them with the paddle. I went under. I panicked. I come up. They pushed me under. I was ready to fight. It wasn't very deep but deep enough to scare me. Everyone

was joking and laughing and so I mellowed out. I had my fun with
them and they were just getting even. That was their fun. We stayed
in the potato house that night. Roger's barn [the Haley farm on East
Presque Isle Road in Caribou] has wooden ventilators that go part-
way in the bins and that lets the air get through to ventilate the potatoes. You turn them upside down and they look just like a coffin.
Some of the guys slept in those; others turned them the other way
and slept on them. Some just slept on the floor. We made it through
the night. Me and my big mouth. One other brother-in-law slept in
the front of the potato house with me. We got up in the morning,
and not thinking, someone asked me how I slept through. I said,
Fine, except for Gary.

What did he do?

He wouldn't leave me alone. I had to beat him off all night.

Then I couldn't take it back fast enough. Still haven't lived that
down. Everyone starts hollering, Oh, I slept on the wrong end of the
potato house. I should have been up there.

I think the first year Roger took them, Danny was about seven.
Jason, Danny, and Brent went. Jason and Brent were in middle
school. Danny was just starting school. Poor Sherrill didn't want to
let Danny to go. Then they talked her into it, so she let Danny go.
Not to sound nasty or anything, but Danny got horny for the first
time on his trip with Roger. They got to a hunting camp and they
were starting to get supper. Well, the other boys picked on Danny a
little bit. They locked him in the outhouse and he couldn't get out.
He started crying, so Roger corrected the other two boys and
brought Danny in and told him to get up on the top bunk and read a
comic book or something. When he got up there and threw himself
back, he hit his head. When he looked, there was deer rack up there.
All of a sudden he started laughing. Roger couldn't figure out what
he was laughing at. Danny, what's so funny?

Danny said, Look at me—I'm horny.

They took pictures of that and had to bring it home to show Sherrill. He still gets teased about that, too. Sherrill said, My poor little baby. He's in college now.

Roger used to work for Dickie Smith. We actually made Dickie speechless one day. They had what they called the Triple Crown farm wave.

BARB: I helped out there in the fall. Every time the guys would see each other, they'd all give the middle finger. And I said, What is that, the Triple Crown farm wave or what?

STUART: Or we'd say, How are you, you old son of a whore? Someone come up from down below, they'd think you hate each other, the way you talk to each other.

We were helping Roger out one year. It was kind of a frosty morning. We couldn't do anything, so it was kind of slow. So they decided to dig one trip. Well, they had Dickie start to dig. I'd been running the windrower, so I made my trip. Then Dickie was following down through with his harvester. We were about through the field and he gives me the Triple Crown farm wave, gives me the finger. I just turned around and dropped my pants and mooned him. Everyone was rolling and laughing. Dickie just pulled his hat down and shook his head. Never heard nothing out of Dick the rest of the day. Didn't talk to me, didn't come near me. He was running the harvester that year too, with his arm in a sling.

That was my first year running the windrower and he showed me how to do it. He drove me a trip and showed me how to run it and explained it. I said, Okay, I think I can do it.

On the next trip, I was driving it by myself. Dick was out walking next to it. He started reaching over it and I stopped. He said, No, no, I'm fine, keep going. Don't stop.

I said, Okay.

Stuart, Barb, Janelle, and Jason, June 14, 2002

Started it and kept going again. All of a sudden, I heard something. I turn around and he's wrapped in the windrower. He had a little hole in his coat and the grease fitting caught it and pulled him in. The only thing that saved him—it was a belt drive, and the belt started slipping. It dislocated his arm. I didn't think to shut the tractor off or shut the power-take-off down. I had to get Roger's partner and they got him out of it, but the rest of that fall he worked with his arm in a sling.

Mike says he remembers Dickie Smith, those long legs coming down the field, and his falling asleep in the truck on the side of the road.

Barb had just gone through a hysterectomy. I got her a TV for her bedroom, so we had two remote controls. I come home from work, she'd play a trick on me or I'd change the channel on the TV and she had the other remote and she'd change it. I couldn't quite

191

figure it out but then I did. Wayne and his son Ben came over one afternoon just to visit. Ben loves TV and was sitting on the couch with the TV remote. The other remote happened to be there, so I picked it up and they didn't see me. Ben changed the channel and I'd go down two or three. He'd go back where it was and I'd go back down. We did that five or six times. Pretty soon Wayne saw that Ben was having trouble with it and asked what was going on. I don't know. I change the channel, it goes where I want it, and then it goes down two or three. Wayne sassed him a little bit and corrected him and said, It's gotta work. It's just a remote. You must be doing something wrong.

So, when Wayne did it, I did the same thing to Wayne. Well, I got Wayne three or four times. Barb saw what I was doing. She started laughing and it made Wayne mad once he figured out what was going on. He said, Come on, Ben, let's go.

Lance, Janelle and Madison

BARB: I love April Fools' and I live for April Fools' Day. This one year I had to get my brother-in-law because he's always getting me, and nobody ever gets him. It was April Fools' morning and I'm trying to think, What could I say? What could I say? Stuart and I were talking. I know what.

I was working at The Jade as a cocktail waitress and also at State Farm Insurance. At the time, one of the girls at State Farm was getting done and there was a little party for her the night before. I called Terry at home and my sister Sharon answered the phone. She was just as sick as could be. You're not feeling good, eh?

No.

I'm actually calling for Terry if he's home.

No, he's working. What do you need?

I'm thinking, do I do this to her or not? I said to myself, Oh, what the heck.

Sharon, I went out with the girls last night and we went to The Jade and I drank too much and I got caught for OUI on my way home. I'm in Caribou jail right now and I have a choice: I can go to Houlton and spend 48 hours and do my time or I can go home and go later. So, I'm going to Houlton. Would you go tell Stuart where I am? He's still home with the kids. I don't dare to call him.

Oh, I'll go in and tell him.

No, no, no, Sharon, you don't have to. That's all right. I'll call him.

No, I'll go in.

Sharon, no—you know what today is?

No, what?

April Fools'!

Ooooh. She could hardly talk. I could hardly hear her voice. I thought, I got her. I was happy. I was all excited that I had done that, so I go and take a shower. All of a sudden, I could hear Terry's voice in the kitchen. The bathroom door opens and Stuart says, The old drunk's in there. Go get her.

Terry didn't come in. Oh, my God, Terry's at the house. Stuart called me an old drunk. What's this all about? So, I hurry up and get out of the shower, go out in the kitchen and Sharon and Terry are out there. Terry said, She looks okay.

I said, Yeah, why? I'm fine.

Aw. April Fools'!

My sister drove into his mechanic shop where he was working on a trailer truck. He was grease from head to toe. She told him I got caught for OUI, that he had to bail me out. He had come to the house, thinking he was going to fend for me and get me out of jail. The worst of it was, the garage is also a liars' location where all the locals go and gossip. There was Uncle Roland, Nason, Glenn, and Arnold Haines. They all heard Sharon say I got caught for OUI, was drunk and in jail and then the joke was on me because it was probably spread all over Aroostook.

STUART: Terry's kind of like Dickie. He was all grease. When he came to talk about it, he was all gentleman and serious and he'd only come so far into the house. He'd lean through and talk. Once he realized he'd been had, his mouth dropped clear to the floor. He turned around. He couldn't believe he'd been had. If he'd known that when she was in the shower, he'd have gone right in.

BARB: I thought, holy, am I lucky he didn't come in.

STUART: Wasn't *he* lucky.

BARB: Then he'd have been fooled twice.

They got Stuart's mom the same year. Told her the same joke, only it backfired. I said Stuart was the one that got caught. Oh, my God, I thought she was going to have a heart attack on the telephone.

Oh, my goodness, he's going to lose his job. What did he do that for?

This was Stuart who really does no wrong. She was just about in tears and I said, Ardith, it was an April Fools' joke.

Ooh, you're the worst daughter-in-law I've ever had!

She's only got two. This wasn't funny. I know I couldn't joke with his mother, but on Terry it worked out well. He's always tried to get me since and hasn't.

That was one-on-one brother-in-law. The other brother-in-law, Sean, one year he got Joan a refrigerator from Sears. He procrastinated and got it Christmas Eve. Well, they couldn't deliver, so he decided to take it himself. He has a little short-bed Toyota pickup. He picked it up and started home. It fell off between Presque Isle and Fort Fairfield. Nobody stopped to help him but he got it back on the truck and got over here to Fort Fairfield. He called a friend, Mike Beaulieu, to come over and help him take it in the house. They tried to take it in the house and the door was too narrow, so they had to take the hinges off the door and also off the refrigerator. It got scratched going through the doorway. After they got it inside the house, they pull out the other refrigerator; go to put this one in there and the cupboard was too low. They had to shave some off. Sean was shaving off some at the bottom of the cupboard. They go to put the refrigerator in and it must have hit the cupboard. The cupboard breaks and Joan's wedding dishes fall and break. Joan walks in.

STUART: And he's still alive!

BARB: Two years later, I thought, I got to get Sean because he's quite the prankster. I made a little ad for the *Fort Fairfield Review* and it said:

FOR APPLIANCE DELIVERY SERVICE

PLEASE CALL SEAN BERNARD

The girl at the newspaper knew Sean and just loved this story, so she found the cutest little picture of this little guy pushing this refrigerator. We were going to put his real phone number but we decided to use a fake number. He got a lot of calls but they didn't answer their phone that night. It was pretty good. So, that's how I got Sean.

STUART: It's hard to get Sean because he got us, too. One year the Campbells all drew names for Christmas. I got Mary's name. Thirty dollars was the limit that we could spend on each other. I made the big mistake. I told Barb I had to spend more than that on her mother. Barb went out with me and we got a really nice dress. We come here

Thirteen *is* a Lucky Number

Mimi, Madison, and Grampy

Christmas Day. She went around telling everyone, Wait until you see the present Stuart got Mom. You're really going to like it, this and that.

If she'd been quiet nothing would have happened. Then it come time to open the presents. All of sudden, Sean made a big deal, saying, Everyone come and see what Stuart got Mary.

She opened it up and it was ashes inside a round box. Sean had taken her sister Janet and they went upstairs and they switched. Mary looks at me like, are you trying to tell me something? She said, Are these my ashes?

MARY: Of all the in-laws and children, he's the last one I expected it from.

STUART: I looked at Barb. What the hell's going on? Where did the dress go?

She didn't know. She said, Stuart, what did you do?

I don't know.

Janet said, It wasn't my idea.

Sean's over in the corner busting a gut laughing.

Hey, Stuart, what did you get Mary?

So, after that, whenever Sean got Mary some scallops and lobsters from the Fish and Game Club, he'd say, What did you do?

I'd say, We got her ashes.

CHAPTER FIFTEEN

Gary

*I did the wash one day. Remember that? We had one of those
old-time wringer washers. Pat was putting towels in, so I went
and put my hand in it. It went clear up to my shoulder.*
      ~Gary

GARY: Even though I'm number six to be born, the number 13
keeps showing up. Other 13s are my oldest son Anthony, who was
born December 13. Alan was born June 13.

They found me in the ditch. I was told I was adopted.

Lisa [Beaulieu] and I live in Grand Isle where I am a member of
the Volunteer Fire Department. I am a truck dispatcher, office manager, and fill-in truck driver at Morin Farms. Lisa works in the deli
department at Paradis Shop 'n Save in Madawaska.

BOB: He always had pickups all tore apart. He'd have pieces all
over the house. He had himself a girlfriend. They'd ride around and
they'd hang onto one another. They'd come in here. One would sit
down in a chair and then one would sit on the other one. They'd hug
one another and hang on. They did that for about two years. He was
always taking that pickup apart and putting it back together, working
on a pickup.

Amanda, Gary, and Lisa

Gary would never get dirty. He was very, very clean. He used to work down at the First National for four years before they closed. It was First National then. They liked him good down there. He was a good worker. I don't know what happened to him. Now he's never clean.

GARY: Lisa's brother Mike is my friend. Look, I went and married her. Her aunt was the boss at First National. I should have learned from that. She was nasty and they're both alike.

LISA: Mike was always bringing home stray dogs.

GARY: The girls didn't have to do anything. We had to do it. Dishes. I did the wash one day. Remember that? We had one of those old-time wringer washers. Pat was putting towels in, so I went and put my hand in it. It went clear up to my shoulder. We didn't know, so Pat puts it in reverse and backs it out.

BOB: I think it was our neighbor Ida got her tit caught in one. She was having a hard time putting stuff through and she was feeding it, feeding it. When it went through it pulled her shirt in and she got her tit caught in it.

MARY: An old-fashioned mammogram!

We have a picture of Gary when he was two or three years old. He stepped in a hornet's nest. His eyes were shut and his legs were all swollen. Instead of running away he kept jumping up and down. Sam had that on a slide and they showed that every time they came up.

People from Connecticut knew that Sam [Bob's brother-in-law] and Sis had family from northern Maine and they think it's wild country. A bunch of hicks. We had a bathtub on the front lawn that the cows used to drink from. The kids used to swim in it in the summertime. Sam had Bob go out there without a shirt on and took his picture. He told everybody that's where they took their baths. He had more fun with that.

GARY: Roland, Dave and I took the International truck to Connecticut to move Roland and Steffie up here. The body on the

The VW Rabbit

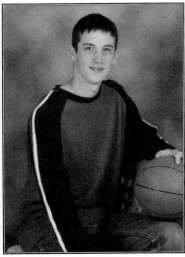

Top left, [Gary's children] Anthony, top right, Alan, bottom left, Amanda Marie

truck was 24 feet long and they had the boat loaded down. We burned three or four wheel bearings off the boat trailer. They told me, Just go down there, you won't have to do nothing. Right! We lugged junk for three days. We'd see stuff falling off here and there.

That reminds me of when we used to ride around in the old army jeep with no floorboards— the one you didn't like us to ride in. Pretty much like a four-wheeler. We never got hurt.

MARY: Oh, that thing. That was dangerous.

Grampy's old VW Rabbit was donated to Dave, then you.

GARY: That thing was wrecked more than once. All of us boys wrecked it at least once. It had the pins on the hood to hold it down. Someone didn't put them in, and it flew off going down Main Street. It had that scoop on the front that hit when you went over something. Cattle catcher.

BOB: They *had* to put that on. You couldn't get your feet in there for wires. Lights here, lights there. Speakers, big speakers.

I took it and went to Madawaska. They told me it was good on gas. There was a half a tank when I left here. I got up there and I still had half a tank. Yeah, it is pretty good. I drove all around up there and I started back. I had plenty of gas. I got fifteen miles out of Madawaska. Bang. It was out of gas. It was cold. It was wicked, wicked cold. I walked to the place of a guy I knew. He got me five gallons and

Alan, Jessica and Anthony

Gary and Amanda

I put that in. I thought that would get me home. I got to Van Buren and it quit. I parked it at Trustworthy Store, called Mary and she came up. We put booster cables on it and still couldn't get it started.

I went up the next morning and we got it going. I got halfway to Caribou and couldn't see a thing. The water came up over and froze to the windshield. We took it to someone's yard and left it there for three weeks. You couldn't work on it, it was so cold. We finally got it home. The gas gauge didn't work. Nothing worked on it. I was a little disgusted with it. I was three days getting that damned thing home. I didn't fool with the boys' cars anymore. I don't know why I even took it.

GARY: We'd ask for a vehicle to go out at night. We had to take the marked car, the Dodge with the Viking Sewing Center sign all over it. Everybody knew where we were.

What were you doing in Mars Hill last night?

Wasn't in Mars Hill.

How come I seen your car there?

So, we learned quick. Don't take that car. Take it to your friend's house and take theirs. That thing was just as bad as the Rabbit. It broke down everywhere you went.

BOB: Dodge. Yeah, right from the day I bought it.

They all had to work when they came home from school. It was quite a lot of chores. They'd have to do an hour, hour and a half.

MARY: They had to do their homework. Gary said, What homework?

GARY: Growing up in a big family, you always had someone to fight with. You couldn't get away with anything. There was always someone seeing you that was pissed off at you for something, and they'd tell on you.

When we lived at the little house, the little girls got the good room. I think all three rooms were as big as this dining room.

CHAPTER SIXTEEN

Michael

*I know that I'm the favorite son. Every time I send Mom any-
thing, I put, "Your favorite son," and she'll figure out who it is.
I'm the forgotten one.*
    ~Michael

MICHAEL: That big photo that's going to be on the cover of the
book—the one with all of us with Mom and Dad—I'm smack-dab
in the middle.

MARY: And he looks the same. He looks exactly the same,
except he has some white hair now.

MICHAEL: Moving to Fort Fairfield was great for me because of
the school and meeting Mary. After we moved in town, I had a much
better social life. I met Mary the week before I graduated. We met on
a track meet. I ran the mile and got fifth in the state that year. Mary
won the trip because her neighbor was a shot-putter and needed a
chaperone—another girl to go with her.

MARY: I chased him for 16 years. It took a lot of convincing.

MICHAEL: There was a lot of water under the bridge for both
of us. I went into the service and she was still in school. We stayed
together until my last year of service.

MARY: I had not dated at all in high school and when I graduated, I moved to Georgia where my sister lived, and still does. The real reason why I went was that Michael was in Jacksonville, Florida. My sister's in-laws had a beach house only an hour from his base. We saw each other once in a while for a couple of years. We never really spent a lot of time together at all.

It was a very passionate love affair and then it was long distance. He went out to sea for his six-month journey. I decided to move back to Fort Fairfield and that was the turning point of our relationship. I think it was Christmas that did you in.

MICHAEL: Christmas did me in?

Wedding Day: Mary, Zachary and Michael

A fresh new day, and it is ours,

a day of happy beginnings

when we, Mary Margaret Nightingale

and Michael Paul Campbell

pledge our love as one

on Sunday, the twenty-eighth of December

Nineteen hundred and ninety-seven

at two-thirty in the afternoon

The Northeastland Hotel

Presque Isle, Maine

Cocktails and Hors d'oeuvres

from three until four in the afternoon

MARY: Yes. We had dated almost four years at that point and I got a pair of earrings and a Miss Piggy doll. That's when I decided it was probably time to move on. I was expecting a ring and I got earrings.

Thirteen *is* a Lucky Number

We kind of went our separate ways, although I probably should have mentioned that we were going separate ways. I kind of left that out. While he was gone, I won Miss Maine and when he came back, I was getting ready for the Miss America Pageant. I was actually not allowed to see him. It was right after Vanessa Williams's reign and scandal, so they didn't allow the candidates to date. They knew that Michael and I had had a long history and they were just being cautious. Miss Maine contest is a lot different now. Zach tells his friends that his mother was Miss Maine and they laugh.

In 1973 my sister Betty won Miss Maine Teenager. Then she won Miss National Teenager and traveled all over the U.S.

Mary and Saré

Being Miss Maine affected me in several ways. If you were in a job interview and a man is interviewing you, it's a positive thing. If a woman is interviewing you, it's not so positive. Women are jealous. Men are fascinated by it. Now, I don't put it down on my resumé anymore, it's been so long. I obviously used it when I was younger.

MICHAEL: I was absolutely fascinated by it! But that was a rough time for me.

MARY: He was not happy because he couldn't see me.

I started seeing other boys and met my first husband right about that time. I knew him in high school and he was a year older than Michael. We got married and then divorced a couple years later.

Every few years Michael and I would run into each other and have a couple of dates. He would say, Nope, it's not going to work.

I had my son Zach, and that was hard for Michael. We did that for about eight years on and off. Then, we went about two years without seeing each other.

I was home for the Potato Blossom Festival and went to the big dance at the Armory. At this point, I was teaching music in New Hampshire. I had gone back to college after my divorce and got my degree. I graduated when Zach was five.

I was at the dance and my brother Matthew kept saying, Michael is over there.

I said, I know he's over there, and I don't care. I don't want to get hurt. I've tried. I've done all I can do.

Then by the last dance, somehow, I made my way over toward him. I don't know how that happened. He asked me to dance, and it was a slow song. He looked at me and said, I still love you.

I said, I love you too, and we're too old for this.

So, it took about six months before he'd move to New Hampshire. He moved down in February and got a job. Actually, he wanted to back out, too. He had thought it through and about

Thanksgiving time, he said, Nope, this isn't going to work.

I said, This is your last time.

We were married in Presque Isle. Pat and Wayne were in Germany. And Susan wasn't there. Zach was eight years old at the time. And now, Zach is a senior and will be graduating.

MICHAEL: He spent the wedding night with us.

MARY: Yes, I knew I had married the right guy.

Zachary was shocked, I think. I remember him saying to me, I have 60 new relatives!

Michael said Zach had a lost look on his face that day, and he took care of him. We had a party at my parents' house after the wedding, and Zach was supposed to stay with my parents, but my mother was very ill. So, it was either that or have him stay at his Adams grandparents', who also live in Fort Fairfield. Michael said, Why don't we just take him with us. So, he spent the first night with us because he was kind of lost.

MICHAEL: He and I are very, very close.

MARY: Now we have a daughter and that was also my doing. We had talked about it and planned it, so I could take the summer off from teaching. Saré is in first grade. She's Daddy's girl. They go fishing.

MICHAEL: Yesterday we caught about 20 fish and threw them back.

I do carpentry on summer homes in a lake region around Moultonboro. I'm a foreman for Cormack.

MARY: I've been told by his boss that Michael's one of the best carpenters he's ever had. He's very meticulous. He will work on one spot for days to get it right. He does beautiful, beautiful work.

MICHAEL: Our first house was 100 years old. It had a lot of charm but it was a lot of work.

MARY: It took every weekend and all of our money.

Mike and Saré

MICHAEL: We sold that and bought a five-year-old house and it's been great.

MARY: I taught music for six years and then I got a job with GlaxoSmithKline Pharmaceuticals. I'm an executive sales representative. I travel during the day. I'm home almost every night. There are periods when I'm away.

When I first took the job, I left for five weeks of training. Saré was about a year old. Michael was alone the whole summer with her. She didn't even know me, and wouldn't come to me when I came home. He got her off the bottle, and she was sick with ear infections, so it was a hard summer for him.

MICHAEL: When I was growing up, going to the Guerrettes' camp on Mud Lake was a big thing—13 kids on the way to the lake in the station wagon, with coolers, and float tubes.

213

Mike and his two Marys

One time, Dad wasn't with us and Mom was driving. A cop stopped us and told her we were overloaded.

Mom said, Yes, I know.

He said, All right.

And we kept going. There wasn't much she could do. It was great times. Aunt Toni and her kids, Curtis and Michele, were there, too.

In the little house on the farm, there were five of us in our bedroom—Jim, me, Sue, Roberta, and Joan. Janet wasn't born yet. The rest of the older kids slept upstairs. I guess you'd call it an attic. The room that we were in was probably eight by ten feet. Very small.

I remember there was a hill from the barn to the house. In the wintertime, we had gotten a toboggan for Christmas, so the boys were piled on the toboggan and were sliding down the hill toward the house. We ran into the house, full bore! Dave was in the front and he got smushed into the house. It made such a bang, Mom came running out to see what was going on.

Another memory is about Grampy and Grammy Campbell, who lived in the house at the top of the hill, 30 feet away. They used to watch us younger kids when the older ones were working in the fields. I remember peanut butter and butter sandwiches that Grammy used to make for us. I've never had them anywhere else. And she fried donuts for us.

MARY: I could make you some peanut butter and butter sandwiches.

MICHAEL: I remember the ice cream truck but I didn't work on it. It was the younger girls. They went to the air base, so it worked better having girls sell.

MARY: When they make the movie, I want to play the older me. The movie would be an up-and-downer.

MICHAEL: I had Grampy Campbell's old car after they took his license away, and Dave did the auto-body work. Grampy had smashed it up pretty good. Dave was a budding auto body guy, so he put a spoiler on it, all that kind of stuff on the VW Rabbit. That's what we drove around. I drove it back and forth when I worked at Burger King. And if you went fast enough the hood would kind of lift up a little bit.

I remember the fire. It was pretty traumatic. I was there. It was a sleet, hail, and ice storm. I think that losing the animals was the worst thing. Dad had had a really good farming year before the fire and had purchased a lot of equipment. A lot of it was in the barn.

MARY: When they had their sewing store in Madawaska, my mother's shoe store was on the other side of it. They shared a building with two storefronts. My mother also had a shoe store in Presque Isle, called Ernestine's Ladies Discount Shoes.

Michael's mother made the dress I wore in the Miss Fort Fairfield Pageant. It was lilac taffeta. Then, I wore it to my senior prom. My

Mike and Saré, 2003 festival

mom would get material, we'd go over. Mary made a lot of clothes for me. And she made my parents' curtains for their whole house.

MICHAEL: I think Mary and I almost met when we were really young. They had a dog that they didn't want. It wasn't behaving right or something. She lived in town and we lived out on Green Ridge. We didn't go to the same school. They brought the dog out to Dad to see if he wanted it.

MARY: His dad worked for my dad at the university. That was Brownie. We had to keep him chained and it was bark, bark, bark.

MICHAEL: He was the best dog we ever had, actually.

MARY: My grandmother and grandfather used to live across the street from Michael's family when they moved to Fort Hill. My grampy was very hard of hearing. I think I heard the story that Michael's family could hear my grandmother yelling.

I remember my grandmother saying, You wouldn't believe what moved in across the street.

MICHAEL: We moved in on a flatbed farm truck with furniture and all the stuff piled on it. And kids on top of that.

MARY: My grandmother was very proper. She was collected. She was Canadian and big into the Queen.

MICHAEL: We were like the Clampetts.

MARY: I knew Michael's sisters Susan and Roberta. Susan was in my class. When I started chasing him after that track meet, of course, I became really good friends with Susan, to get into the house. Susan, Roberta, and I hung out the last couple years of high school. I knew of Michael. He was the older guy. He didn't pay any attention to me, and I didn't pay any attention, until later.

Mary, Saré and Michael

I used to go up at dinnertime. His mother cooked in huge pots, just gigantic pots of food. I can remember Bob sitting in the chair, reading the newspaper, and chaos is going on around him. He's just sitting there as if no one is in the room. It was always just full of people.

I'd go back to my house. I'm the youngest of five. By the time I got to high school I was alone, so it was like I was an only child. It was very quiet at my house.

After Michael and I got together we'd go for brief visits at his house and then go back to my parents' house, which was a lot quieter, and a lot less kids running around. When the kids were younger, you can just picture it.

MICHAEL: My parents used to work very, very hard. For quite a while, they worked eight to eight, when they had the sewing center. We didn't see them a whole lot during that time. I was at their house the night they won the Megabucks. Dad had just watched it on TV. He said, I think I just won the Megabucks.

I said, Right, yeah, right.

He says, Mary, get over here.

They looked at the numbers and sure enough, they had won.

MARY: I remember my mother calling me in Wells, saying, You'll never guess who won the Megabucks.

MICHAEL: Dad tried farming for a couple of years while they had the sewing machine business. I was the one who had to go out after school and do the spraying.

MARY: His family has a bunch of men who, besides Bob, won't speak unless you drag it out of them.

Michael has been a wonderful father to Zach. I said to Zach the other day, You do know that Michael loves you, don't you, even thought he doesn't say it?

He said, I know. Mom, it would be weird if he said it.

Tri-state Megabucks winner Robert Campbell of Fort Fairfield and wife, Mary, with first of 20 installments on $500,000 lottery prize. (Ketch photo)

Former Caribou man half-million $ richer

by Beth Ladner

"I only buy a ticket once every three weeks," said Robert Campbell, co-winner of this week's $1 million Tri-State Megabucks jackpot. "In fact, I didn't buy this ticket until six o'clock Saturday night. I'm tickled to death."

Campbell and his wife, both of Fort Fairfield, were in Augusta Monday to claim the first installment of their $500,000 prize. "We'll be getting a check for $18,750 for the next 19 years. Not bad, eh?" he exclaimed.

"I bought the ticket at Hedrich's Market in Fort Fairfield," he said. "I'm really glad for the owner because he's just starting out and this will help him out a lot," he added. "I think this will do a lot for Aroostook County, too."

Campbell and his wife were watching the drawing on television when he discovered he had won. The numbers 3-9-12-14-23-33 have changed his life for the better, he said.

"The first thing we did was buy a new van we had had our eye on," he said. "My wife is going to be opening a drapery monograming shop, too. This will be a good suppliment to our income, especially with 13 kids, five of them in college."

Campbell, 50, split the jackpot earnings with Paulette Hill, a chambermaid, from Hyde Park, Vt.

"This will definately make life a little easier," Campbell concluded.

Campbell and his family are former Caribou residents.

October 26, 1987 Winning Day! From the Aroostook Republican

My family says, I love you. After Bob had his stroke, I remember saying to Michael, You should tell him you love him, and he did. I think it was a shock.

Very opposite families. We're very affectionate in my family. We hug and kiss every time we see each other and say we love each other when we talk on the phone. His family is totally the opposite. Michael, believe it or not, is very affectionate with Saré and me, too. And the dog, which he's patting right now.

I always kiss and hug Bob and tell him he's looking handsome. I'm the one who challenges Bob when I see him. He's right and I'm right. We both like attention. We're alike that way.

MICHAEL: I told Mom a few times that I love her. She likes to hug. I know that I'm the favorite son. Every time I send Mom anything, I put, "Your favorite son," and she'll figure out who it is. I'm the forgotten one.

MARY: Over the years there has been discussion about the favorite daughter-in-law. I'm the favorite daughter-in-law who lives the farthest away. I'd have to say that Sherrill has been the daughter-in-law the longest. Sherrill and I will have to compete for this, I guess.

CHAPTER SEVENTEEN

Roberta

*That's how I learned how to drive. He just left me there with
the keys!*
   ~Roberta

Kim lived with us in Georgia when David and I first got married. Kim and I both did some modeling. But I had to stop and get a
real job. I haven't seen Kim's baby yet. That's one of the bad things
about being down here.

I went to school for a reason, not to model. I went to Bauder
Fashion College in Atlanta, Georgia, and modeling was a required
course the first year I was here. Originally, that was how I got into
it. Then, when my husband took the job with the government, he
had to go back and get his master's degree at Georgia Tech. We had
to move back to Atlanta for a year, so the modeling was something
to do in between my jobs. And prior to children.

My older sisters did not play basketball. Sharon was in the work
program at school, so she worked right from the get-go from high
school on at the same place for 33 years. She's amazing—the things
that she has done and accomplished.

I think Barb played a little bit of basketball, but again, she wanted
the job thing so she could *tool* the silver car—the Silver Fox. My

Joan, Kim, Janelle, Jennifer, Roberta, Susan, Janet

mom had a silver Grand Marquis and Barb used to *tool* in it, and she'd have to go get groceries or do whatever. She'd take Sue and I. We five were the little girls but we were the medium girls. That's what Sue and I always called ourselves. For Barb to be able to go to town from the farm, she'd always have to take us. Then we'd *tool* up and down the road from Burger Boy back down to McDonald's and down through Caribou. She needed money to do that. Also, because we were on the farm, we didn't have rides back and forth. We'd have to get on the bus.

I played basketball in third, fourth, and fifth grades at Zippel School in Presque Isle. In third grade, I had to play with boys because they didn't have a girls' program. When we moved to Fort Fairfield, I was able to start right up because I was in sixth grade at Fort Fairfield Middle School. My coach was Mrs. Wilbur, and she was another great person, like my high school coach Mrs. Peters.

Brandon, David, Roberta and Zachary

We went from sixth grade up to eighth grade, and I had the same group of girls—Robin Davenport and Sherry Finnemore—playing with me. We were the trio, always captains together in all

Spencer Robert

sports: field hockey, softball, volleyball, and basketball. Dad said, Anything that had a ball, I chased it!

That's probably why I like dogs. I currently have three.

I was six foot tall by eighth grade. Just before I turned 13, I went into my freshman year and I was the tallest person in the class. I

223

Sue, 1983

had found out about field hockey tryouts. I went up there two weeks prior to school starting. They had actually already started, and Mrs. Peters had the team out running. So, I had already missed a week but she let me do a walk-on. The team had already been picked. Even though I was late, she let me on. She felt sorry for me. And that's how I got started with Mrs. Peters. Both Mrs. Peters and Ken were good people to be with kids.

Sue was very athletic also, but she was a runner and she skied. She was on the Fort Fairfield cross-country team and they went to Sugarloaf. It was her first year of skiing and she got going really, really fast. She was so excited because she was beating everybody. She passed everybody. All of a sudden, there was a big turn and that's why everybody was slowing down. They knew it was coming and she didn't, so she kept her momentum and ran into a tree. She got banged up but no broken bones or anything like that. She really

Mémère and Sue

wanted to do well with that because she had done so well running. She met Chester then, who also ran and skied.

Thomas, Kaitlyn and Jordan Cyr

My freshman year of basketball, Kirsten Pendleton fouled out, so I got to go in and shoot foul shots. We beat Orono and that made us go on to the Eastern Maine Tournament. Another one of those nerve-wracking moments. And I would do it all again!

My boys were going through my yearbook the other day. They said, You had a good childhood. You've got pictures everywhere.

Thirteen *is* a Lucky Number

Roberta

The work ethic I learned from my parents has followed me throughout my life. I cannot tell you how many bosses have said, I don't know who taught you how to work, but they taught you right.

I learned to drive in the ice cream truck. I had driven tractors and lawn mowers but I had never driven a stick shift, per se. Dad brought Pete home and told me I needed to drive it out to Grampy and Grammy Campbell's house. That's how I learned to drive. He just left me there with the keys! It has the starter and clutch and the four pedals across there. I learned! And I probably drive better than most men. Pete was definitely a male vehicle, and I'd have to say that I dated him for two summers. We didn't keep the money we got from selling ice cream. It went to my parents and they provided me with my sports equipment. And my sports were not cheap.

I still don't know how my parents did all that they did, now that I have three of my own—13 kids in 14 years. That's how I talked my husband into having my second child. I told him at this age my mom already had 10 children. It's time for me to have my second.

When I first met David he asked what my name was, and I told him Roberta. He told me that it had to be one of the ugliest names. He asked me some of my sisters' names. So, I started naming them. He said, My God, didn't your parents know any normal names?

He hated Janet and Joan. He said Pat, Sharon, and Barb were just old names. He said Sue was okay. But then when I said Kim, he called me Kim for about three weeks because he couldn't stand my name. At the time I was actually going by Bert, and he didn't want to be dating a boy. I am named for my dad. Add an "a" to his first name and an "e" to his middle name: it's Robert Louis and Roberta Louise. He had five boys and four girls and he had to wait for me to do that ugly name. But now David calls me Roberta.

The son-in-law talk was a given with Dad. David said it wasn't as bad as he expected, but he was expecting something different. David's not around Dad but a few times out of the year, or every few years, so he does not know the score.

I know Dad thinks kids should stay in their hometown, but it depends upon the profession. There is not an engineering job up there for David. If you're not happy in your job, you're not going to be happy.

Roger stopped here recently on a run down to Florida. Brandon just turned 13 and when he saw Roger, he asked me why

Spencer Robert, Zachary and Brandon

Thomas, Grampie, Mary, Jordan, Sue

Roger was shrinking. I told him that Roger was not shrinking. It's just that when you were little, you were looking up at him. This time he touched the top of the door casing. But now that Brandon's getting taller, it seems like Roger is shrinking.

Both Grammy and Grampy Campbell were tall. Kim and I are Grammy Campbell made over. Kim has her feet. We both wear size 10 like Grammy did, but Kim has ugly feet like Grammy's. She used to soak her feet. Oh, I hated to see those feet. She had some medical problems and had some toes amputated. And she had corns. We didn't get any height from Mom's side, but we got our naiveté from her.

One of the best things that I was able to participate in was when we went to southern Maine to go shopping and to the Ice Capades—to be there with Mom and her sisters, and hear their stories, and some of the things they did. Sue, Barb, and I don't have anything to worry about. They did some things, too. My mom has a certain sense of humor. After hearing them, I see where a lot of it comes from.

CHAPTER EIGHTEEN

Janet

I'm glad I was at the end of the family because I was able to
watch and learn from all my older brothers and sisters.
~*Janet*

Hello! I'm Janet Helen Campbell Giberson. I filled the egg carton—number 12, that is, out of 13. I don't think I would change one thing about our life. Growing up in a large family is a gift all in itself. I remember when I was young, wishing I had this or that (just objects) that some of my friends had. But even though my friends had a lot of objects, they were very empty emotionally or spiritually. We may not have had many things, but we had the best home life. Life is what you make it. We always had food on the table. Our parents were always home. All of our siblings and their families always came over to visit on Sundays. On many Sundays at Mom and Dad's on Fort Hill, it could have been just hours of sitting, talking, laughing or leg wrestling. Mom usually beat everyone. We played many games like Rummikub, Uno, or Yahtzee. It didn't matter the age, everyone played. We were all winners. We would be laughing so hard we had tears in our eyes. We may have been a little tired, too. We enjoyed each other as we still do to this day. It may not be as often, but we make it a point to get together as often as we can.

Thirteen *is* a Lucky Number

My parents are wonderful people. To raise 13 children on their own, without state assistance, is a true sign of two people who aren't afraid of work, aren't afraid to sacrifice, and are willing to give up a lot of their own time. Mom and Dad are definitely workaholics, but you know, it shows in every one of us. We have all worked for everything we have. Dad made sure we always had something to do. He also made sure that we treated all people with respect, especially the elderly. He expected us to look appropriate, particularly going to a job. We always thought he was just a nag. I guess all of his nagging paid off, because we are all very well liked, respected, and known as hard workers, just like our parents. Another gift that we received from our parents was to be caring and generous. Other people usually come before ourselves. There is always a way you can help someone out. It can be as simple as smiling at someone and saying hello. I love to laugh. As you know, I usually have a smile on my face. I can't imagine life any other way. So, usually if I see people not smiling, I try to get them to smile just a little. A smile is like good medicine and it's free of charge. Or it could be letting someone stay with you while they are going through rough times.

I love people. I like to meet new people or help people out. To me every day has a purpose, if not for myself, for someone else who could use a little assistance. I'm never bored because if I have all my stuff caught up, I'm always up to helping someone else. I really feel we all have that quality of caring. I see it in my parents, especially Mom, and I've seen my brothers and sisters show this quality many times throughout their lives. I'm glad I was at the end of the family because I was able to watch and learn from all my older brothers and sisters.

I began babysitting at a young age. Sharon's oldest is only six years younger than I am. I got to really know my older sister Sharon when I babysat for her. She was married when I was five, so Sharon's children are close to me in age and in friendship. There's another great thing about a big family: You always have a friend. I do have lots of friends, but it seems most of my life is with my family—my best friends.

Something we do very well is get along. Our neighbor Charlie Lockhart said, Now, I've lived next to you for a long time. You always got along outside the house, having fun playing games. He asked, Did you get along inside, too?

Honestly and proudly I could always say yes. Very seldom did we fight. Dad used to make us (the older ones, usually Barb and Gary) hug and kiss if we got into a fight. I use the same tactic on my kids. It works. It's going to be a long life if you are always fighting. Hug and kiss. It brings a smile to your face.

The last five were all girls: Sue, Bert, Joan, Janet, and Kim. Mom used to dress us alike. We had gauchos with vests, which she made herself, of course. We always shared a bedroom. We were known as the five little girls. We have done a lot of fun things together.

It was the eighth grade prom. Bert had wicked thick hair. So, she wanted her hair cut for the prom. Her date was Mark Giberson, who's now my husband. The funny thing is that she wanted her hair layered by her ears. That was the new look. It was straight across. Bert's hair stuck out. It was the ugliest. We all went Oooooo— for prom night. They went to the prom together, and I ended up marrying him.

Janet and Mark, September 18, 1993

231

Thirteen *is* a Lucky Number

Janet, the best mail carrier in The County

As you may have noticed, we aren't ones to brag much or talk about ourselves. We just do what needs to get done and then you move on. Most of us find it hard to write down our thoughts or feelings because it is not in our nature. We never really discussed personal issues, and we respected each other's privacy.

Speaking of privacy, I find it so funny that in this current time, a house has to have two bathrooms or more, as well as one bedroom for each person. When we lived on Fort Hill we had one bathroom. The shower was before you went into the bathroom. Mom had made a little yellow curtain that we hung up on two little nails on the door case. If this curtain was up, everyone knew someone was in the shower. So, if you needed the bathroom, you said, Going through, or something like that.

Hard to believe that we all could use one bathroom. Sacrifice, generosity, going without. Some people think that's horrible. They are wonderful gifts. I think the less people use, the happier they might be, if they would only try. A simple life is a happy life.

I graduated from Fort Fairfield High School in 1987. I was very involved in the school, pretty much anything I could join. I was in all the sports, chorus, National Honor Society, Junior Exhibition, Miss Fort Fairfield Pageant, French Club. I loved to help with any dances, decorating, setup, and cleanup; bottle drives, car washes—anything to help out our class. We had a fun class. We liked to sing and dance. We all got along quite well.

After high school I went to Maine State Academy of Hair Design in Portland. I got my cosmetology license and worked in Caribou at Images for a year. My hands became irritated, so I got done.

I wanted to be an interior designer. I wanted to go to California, go to school. I'm practicing as I go, and after I retire from the post office, I'll have a second career.

I've been a mail carrier for 14 years. I started part-time in Fort. Went to Presque Isle for four years. I filled in down to Houlton. Now I'm back here. I love it. I like being outdoors. I love people, so it's perfect. I get exercise. I'm outside.

As you know, I love to talk and I have lots of energy to burn, so getting out and walking every day and seeing people is a perfect place

Janet and Sis

Kayla, Janet, Nicole, Mark and Christopher

for me to be, not to mention, I get to go right home for lunch. Extra bonus. That's when I get the house picked up or do my little things. You can get a lot done in a half hour when no one else is home.

Dad says I could be a racetrack announcer. What he's getting at: I talk fast. I walk a mile a minute. I talk fast. I walk fast. There's a hundred things going on in my head.

I am not really a sit-down person. I always have something going on. If it's not my own project, I'll be helping someone else with theirs. I love doing yard work and playing in the dirt. I have become a true lover of flowers. We have made quite a few flower beds at our house. We just finished one last week [September]. The kids love to help, too. Actually, the girls each have their own flower garden. They pick out their own flowers and plant them. I'm usually the one who takes care of them the rest of the year, but all three enjoy the flowers. They help when we ask and they are proud when people compliment them on the yard. It's a wonderful feeling. Gardening is very rewarding and fulfilling, and a therapeutic hobby. This summer I helped a few people with their flower beds. Good way to start friendships.

I am 36 years old. I am married to Mark Giberson. We just celebrated our 12th wedding anniversary. Mark is also from Fort Fairfield.

Being part of the Campbell family was scary at first for Mark. After all, he is from a family of four. He was definitely not used to the chaos, noise, commotion, and so many girls. He has adapted well. He is now used to all of our habits and get-togethers. He is happy to be a part of my family, and I am happy to be a part of his family. He is a very nice man and a good father.

We have three wonderful kids: Nicole is nine, Kayla seven, and Chris is six. They are true seeds of Mark and I. Everyone says Nicole looks just like me, Chris looks just like his father, and Kayla is a mix. More like me, I think, especially when she haunts her father.

My husband Mark works at Maine Mutual Group Insurance Company. He has been there for four years. He is an insurance adjuster. He is very good at his job. Before he worked there, he

Thirteen *is* a Lucky Number

b: Sharon, Joan, Roberta, Kim, Mike, Gary
f: Susan, Barbara, Bob, Janet, Mark, Mary, Dave, Jim

worked construction for about 18 years. Our house shows much of his skill—the woodwork, the steps. Each year we do a little work on the house, room by room. This one is the big one though. The kitchen. Can't wait!! The kids and I will stay at Mom and Dad's for a week or so while Mark works late nights in the kitchen.

I also love (or try) to decorate. I love to watch HGTV or any other home improvement show. The kids always look forward to updates, too. They never know what I'm up to. Half the time, I don't either. That's the fun of it. It's a good feeling knowing that we did it ourselves. Our home tells much about us, as do most homes.

I love kids. Besides our three, we seem to always have three or four extra at our house. But it's nice to see kids being kids. Most of the time they don't have the chance to do kid things. They grow up fast. Not only do kids learn from us, but also we adults learn from our kids.

CHAPTER NINETEEN

Kim: The Youngest

It took me until I was thirty to learn that love, family, com-
munication, and all that stuff's way better than money.
~Kim

Kim and Siblings at Bob and Mary's

KIM: I guess being the youngest, I was too young for a lot of things. Joan, Janet, and I were the last three home. We went with Mom and Dad to Mount Katahdin.

The others went to 4-H. I didn't get to go. I remember every year they cleaned the Green Ridge Cemetery and went to the fair.

I remember one time I was going to see Santa Claus. I ate a peach or plum and swallowed the pit. Choked and I couldn't go.

I was too little to go to school.

I think a lot of my memories are with Joan and Janet, with the sports we played.

BOB: The girls used to be quite the thing. They had more crowds for the ball games just to see so many of them play from one family. They were starters. Mike played on the boys' team.

KIM: I was a starter my freshman year. I had to work for it, believe me, with Mrs. Peters. She just retired.

Every summer Mrs. Peters and her husband took the basketball team on a trip down the coast. We tented out. Then they scheduled

Kim the potato peeler

basketball games for three days. You got to rough it out. Mr. Peters drove Dad's van. We went to Eastport and scheduled games with other towns during vacation. It was fun. It makes your team closer, too, when you get to travel like that and live that way. Then you play better together.

MARY: Sue went along and we took Roberta, Robin Davenport, and Sherry Finnemore to basketball camp in Connecticut. I guess the school or Mrs. Peters paid for other camps they went to.

JANET: At the little house one room was full of cribs. The other room was Mom and Dad's, and then upstairs was us. We painted it half pink and half blue, and the girls were on one half, the boys were on the other half. Dad would come up for our *nightly beatings* and he'd tip his head sideways under the eaves and bump his head. Then we'd laugh. He'd say, You think that was funny? I'll do it some more.

KIM: I wasn't born yet. I didn't have a baby picture until I was four.

MARY: I've never heard the end of that.

KIM: In fourth grade I had to do an autobiography. I told Mom I needed a baby picture. So, she gave me one of Sharon. They didn't know the difference.

BOB: When Roger was born, that was when we were fixing the pickers' shack into the little house.

MARY: Bob, it was Barb.

BOB: We were wiring it up, so I went to Sears & Roebuck in Presque Isle to get wiring supplies. Mary, Sharon, Pat and Roger went with me. Sharon came in the store, walked all around. Finally she came over, pulled on my pants and said, Mom's having a baby. She wants you. We went home, dropped the kids off with the hired man, Percy Parker, and took her into Caribou to the hospital. Dropped her off and when I got back home the baby was all born. I thought it was Roger.

Kim and Kevin, married on Magic Island in Honolulu, Hawaii, January 2, 2003

MARY: No, no. It was Barb. They were all born 14 months apart. Roger was born in November. I *know* which one it was. That was the one they charged me for a private room and I slept in the hall for two days. They didn't have any private rooms.

PAT: We were all out front of the farmhouse at the Ashby farm. The steps had metal bars set in cement for railings. We got swinging on them. Barb was eighth grade, or a freshman. Barb said, Watch this. Watch this.

There was plenty of room to go around. She said she'd go backwards. She gave a big push and went right down. She hit her head on the concrete. She landed on her head. We took her into the hospital and the doctor took forever getting there, and the blood was running out. They had towels around her and the blood kept running on the floor—all over.

Another was an accident on a bike. We borrowed the neighbor's bike and it had no brakes. We were racing. Kim said, Are you watching? And she ran into the fire hydrant. Mom and Dad were working in Caribou. Jim put a Band-Aid on it and the blood was gushing.

BOB: I made my bulk truck bodies to fit on the flatbed because I had potato pickers and I had harvesters. I had it so I could use it any way I wanted. When I was putting on the bulk body, I'd put one side on, then the other. The kids would take hold of the stakes, pick up, and put it in there. One stake wasn't going down into the hole. Coburn Morris said he'd move it a little bit with the crowbar so he was pushing it down in. It dropped down in the hole and when it did, he pulled the crowbar back and hit Barb right in the mouth. Broke her front teeth.

MARY: That's probably why Barb's such a nervous mother.

KIM: If we're all on the floor in the same room, Barb thinks the floor is going to cave in, no matter what house you're in—her house, especially.

MARY: I used to have my washer and dryer side by side. There was some vibration.

KIM: Barb wouldn't go in when the clothes were in the washer and dryer. The hot tub's in there, too. She must have dreamt that she fell through the floor.

BOB: Jim and Mike were playing. I had a little Massey Ferguson with a lawn mower on it. Jim was driving it around. Jim stopped and Mike jumped on the back of it. Jim took off going. Mike's foot went down between the fender and the wheel and Mike hollered Whoa, and Jim thought he was saying go. He had hydrostat and he just kept pushing it ahead and giving it more gas. He burned his leg right up. Mike was in the hospital all summer with skin grafts and infection.

Kevin and Kim: expecting

DAVE: I remember I was helping Dad out, doing a heck of a job of tightening up the fenders on the tractor. When I tried to get out of there my ears were stuck. Well, Dad said, we'd have to pull my ears to get me out of there.

BOB: Don't worry about that. I'll put that in fourth gear and drive it down the road. He just pulled his head out and stretched out.

DAVE: Then you made fun of me.

BOB: You should have seen the cars they used to drive. You'd get in and they had wires hanging everywhere. The wire shop wouldn't have as many wires as they had. They had an old VW Rabbit that Dad fixed up. They had speakers in it about the size of that table.

KIM: With pins in the hood. Mike was driving it on Main Street. There goes the hood. Got stopped. Didn't put the pins in, did ya?

BOB: Mike was working at Burger King. He left it up there. Called up one night and said, Dad, you have to come in. The car's down over the ditch.

Well, what?

I don't know. It rolled backwards down over the ditch.

I went in and he'd gone down and fetched up on the exhaust system and bent it right under and he couldn't drive. Well, we used to lug that thing as much as we drove it. We all went in, got hold of it and lifted it up, and got it up out of there.

Then it wasn't too long after we got it going, Jim took it and went to Caribou. He came out by the car wash and couldn't stop, went across the road, and down over the bank. We couldn't sell it, that's what they run with.

KIM: David still has Pete, the ice cream truck—a '56 Chevy that Dad bought from Hugh Pierson and Dave fixed it up.

BOB: They had it nine years and it taught them lots of lessons.

KIM: We took it on base [Loring Air Force Base in Limestone] every day. Dad wouldn't let us go to the barracks, so we sold to the little kids.

BOB: And every day they'd call. We can't get this thing going.

JANET: You had to stop at the gate before going on base, and it'd never fail, I'd always stall it when there'd be people watching. We all knew about the screwdriver and the hammer. You had to hit the carburetor to get it going. I ate a lot of ice cream.

There was a little black guy on base we called Eddie Murphy. Funny as heck. Whenever I'd deliver ice cream, he and his little group of guys always rode their bikes and skateboards and had to do their little tricks.

We went to the Fourth of July [celebration] and were trapped in Trafton Lake with Bert, Barb, and her kids. Bert is a tall blonde. I said to Reggie [Eddie's real name], I want you to meet my sister.

Your sister?

Yeah.

But she's white.

Yeah, so am I. He thought I was black because of my tan. They always told me I was born in the ditch.

KIM: I've always liked money. I worked at Key Bank as a teller. Worked with international banking for six years in Georgia. Then I became a flight attendant.

JANET: She would never be married or have kids, never, ever, ever, ever. Then she turned thirty and realized she could give it up, that money wasn't important.

KIM (holding her new baby, Blake Alexander): It took me until I was thirty to learn that love, family, communication, and all that stuff's way better than money. I felt like playing. Now I work out at DFAS (Defense Finance and Accounting Services). When I was in eighth or tenth grade, I took a test. I said I wanted to be a stewardess, and I finally got to be one when I was twenty-seven. I got that out of my system. I'm glad I waited to have my baby.

MARY: I think 9/11 had a lot to do with her decision. She was living in Pennsylvania at the time, flying out of New York, and she switched flights with another attendant that day—that flight that went to Pennsylvania. It upset her a lot more than she admits. She was very nervous about flying for a while.

We were in Boston on 9/11 and we thought Kim had flown out to Pennsylvania that day. She took a leave of absence and when she went back, they told her she had to live within two miles of the airport instead of living in Maine and commuting.

She looked great as a flight attendant. When we went to Germany to visit Pat and Wayne, Kim joined us, and Pat didn't recognize her.

Kim was a model with Roberta in Georgia. Roberta stayed with it longer than Kim did.

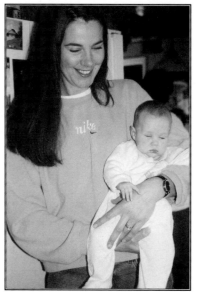

Kim and Jada [Jessica's daughter]

JANET: Kim liked to get checks. We used to clean house for Ruth Anderson. Kim would get checks and she'd never cash them.

KIM: I never got my dividends from the bank because I held onto my checks too long.

I had just graduated. You had to be 19 to go to Canada, so I asked Mom if we could go to the dance at Suzanne's [Joan's classmate is Suzanne LeVasseur].

The next day we were talking about dancing. Mom looks up after listening to us for a half hour. Where did you go last night?

Suzanne's.

LeVasseur?

No, in Canada. They call it Suzanne's. You even asked.

MARY: Where they can drink when they're 19.

245

Thirteen *is* a Lucky Number

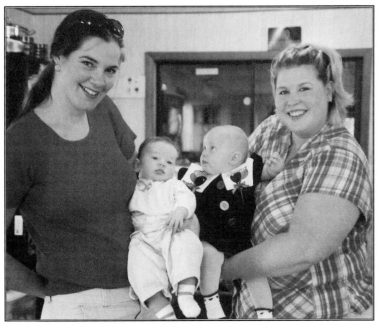

Kim, Blake, Emily and Jennifer

JANET: And you gave me permission. In our heads, we didn't know she was thinking Suzanne LeVasseur's until the next day when we were talking. We were thinking Suzanne's in Canada and she was thinking Suzanne LeVasseur's.

Bert and Sue had been up there. We'd take $10. All we wanted to do was to go dancing. We were the good ones. You heard Barb's stories. They were bad. We were homebodies, really.

MARY: Sharon and Terry had a fire in their trailer Christmas Day 1981. They had been over here and it happened after they got home. They were lucky to get out alive. Lori was the baby and she was inside having a nap. It was an electrical fire started by the fan over the stove. They just barely got Lori out. They had a Christmas tree in the wooden entryway and they were all sitting out there and the kids were playing with their gifts. Everybody thought it was a Christmas-tree fire, but it wasn't.

They moved to Grampy Campbell's old house where they were close to work and babysitters. They bought a house from the base and moved it to their lot. They did it the hard way.

BOB: I always had ten or twelve high school kids working for me. They'd get out there and starting fooling around and I'd tell them, Look, I hired you to work, and you're not going to stand around and talk. I meant it, and when they did it, I gave them particular hell. I didn't go back and tell them the story again. I told them I meant it, and I meant it.

It was the same when we were bringing up the kids. I told them if the neighbor kids did something wrong, it was wrong, and if you do the same thing they did, you're supposed to know better, so you're going to get worse than they did. So, you can remember that. I stuck with that. The other thing was, whatever Mary said to them, I agreed with her, whether I did or not, and she did the same thing with me. We knew we were going to do that when we were going together.

MARY: A lot of times I didn't agree with him, but you can't disagree in front of the children.

BOB: I've never liked hearing a kid cry. I can't stand it. It's okay for a kid to cry if he's hurt. It's natural. When a kid's crying, and he has nothing to cry for, I'd give him something to cry for. A kid crying isn't happy. So, I didn't make him unhappy. I just gave him what he wanted. He wanted to cry, so he had to have something to cry for, so I gave him something to cry for.

Finally, growing up, they knew that they could cry if they wanted to, but they had to have something to cry for. They either had to be hurt or something, not just because they wanted something.

MARY: They weren't whiners. If they fought or got into an argument we'd make them kiss each other, and they had to say they were sorry to each other.

BOB: We started them working from five to six years right on up. They could pull weeds or pick rocks. We had them up at six o'clock, and about noontime we'd go to Echo Lake to play. Not a big reward but it was good that way and we got by real well with them. They knew how to work together. They worked in the potato house on Saturday. They'd say all the other kids have the day off.

We never had to call the kids in the morning. They were always up, did their chores, had their breakfast. The bus came at quarter past seven.

MARY: They had to get ahead for the bathroom. We had one bathroom.

BOB: We never put a curfew.

MARY: We had curfews.

BOB: Well, our curfew was if you went out and you came in at 11 o'clock, you got up at five. If you stayed out to 12 or one o'clock, you got up at four. If they said they were sleepy, I'd say, No, you're not. You weren't tired last night. You can't be that tired now, so you get right up.

If they came in at 10, they got to sleep until six or until they woke up on their own. They didn't lay in bed and sleep any longer. They were always home by 10:30 or 11:00.

If they asked Mary if they could stay out until 12 or one o'clock, and if she thought it was important, she'd say yes. I'd go along if she said yes. If she knew I didn't like it, she'd say no. They'd come ask me. I'd ask, What did Mom say? Well, then that's what I say.

They always had a chance to use vehicles. We always had plenty of vehicles. They'd come and go when they wanted.

Kim, Blake and Kevin, September 2005

BOB: Mary went to Germany to visit Loretta. She was gone for six weeks. Then, we gave her parents the money to go visit Loretta, too. The kids took care of themselves while she was gone. Kim was only four.

PAT: While Mom was gone to Europe for six weeks, the three little ones went down to Grammy Campbell's and Dad didn't even know they were gone.

MARY: When miniskirts were in, Sharon and Pat didn't want to wear their ski pants. It's 40 below and they went on the bus. They would take their skirts and wear them at school. Bob would tell them they weren't dressed warm enough.

BOB: If that bus breaks down, you're not warm enough. So I made up my mind that I was going to be home when the bus came. I locked the door. What's the trouble?

They said, We want to come in.

Nah, you're dressed warm enough for an hour or two. You'll stay there until suppertime.

They cried, cried and then they went out to the barn. They didn't freeze out there.

MARY: They were very upset.

BOB: They wore their pants after that. Just to show them who was boss. I didn't back down on anything. I didn't take no for an answer. Oh, I hate it when a person says, I'll count to seven, then you do this, or I'm going count to 20, and you do this, or three more times and you're going . . . Shut up about it if you ain't going to do it. I didn't care if they didn't like me.

MARY: His philosophy was, I'm their parent, not their friend.

BOB: Now Dave, he was the quiet one, and one you could trust with pretty near anything. He and another boy stole the lunch money at the convent school. The nun collected the money every day and put it in the drawer. Then, she'd turn it in at night. They kept seeing that money and Fish Nadeau's store was over on the corner. They thought they'd take it and she'd never know who did it.

When everyone went out to recess they went in and, somehow, they took the money. She kind of knew who it was, so the nun called us and told us that they took the money. I said, That's all right. We'll take care of that.

When Dave came home, I said, What'd you do today?

Oh, nothing.

Did you go to the store?

No.

Didn't go over and buy stuff?

No.

I said, That's good. I said, You know what I hate? I really hate a thief. But I said, what really makes me boil is a *liar* and a thief. Did you hear what I said?

Yeah.

Now, I'm going to ask you one more time, Was you over to the store today?

Kim the model

Yes, I was.

Buy anything?

Yeah.

Where'd you get the money?

Well, this guy and I took money out of the drawer.

Okay, we'll go in and see the nun and tell her.

No, he didn't want go.

You're going. Took him right in.

He told her, I'm sorry I took the money.

She said, That's nice of you to tell me.

I said, Tell her the truth. Tell her I hate a liar.

Oh, him and I took the money.

Didn't take long to get it out of him, but he knew I meant business right off to start with.

MARY: They didn't get away with too many things.

BOB: Some little things they got away with. Lots of times we knew but we just let it go. It didn't bother us that bad. You have to. But they think they did a great big thing.

MARY: We did the same thing with our parents.

Thirteen *is* a Lucky Number

━━━⟫◆⟪━━━

MARY: Lisa Devine lived with us for two years. Her family was our neighbors out on the farm. How it came about was when her parents separated.

KIM: Mr. Devine moved to Limestone and Mrs. Devine moved to Presque Isle and Lisa wanted to stay in Fort Fairfield so she could graduate with all her friends. I was friendly with her. There were three girls instead of two when she was here.

MARY: She asked if she could live here during the school year. Even before her parents separated, they would bring her to church, and she wanted to come home with us afterwards.

BOB: She was a pretty girl but she wore a lot of makeup, perfumes, and short skirts. I'd say, Lisa, for God's sake, you dress like a French whore. Comb your hair out right and get rid of half of that lipstick and stuff. Put some clothes on.

KIM: We'd say, Go take a shower.

She'd say, I just did!

You stink worse than when you went in.

BOB: I don't know what she'd say to that in a book, but the last time I saw her, she had no makeup, she had her hair combed out straight.

I was just trying to drive it into her head, so she would understand that she was a nice-looking girl, she was a nice girl, she was a smart girl—so what the hell were you doing all that for?

We think the world of Lisa and we always did.

CHAPTER TWENTY

Toni K. Campbell

> *He had one chicken as a special pet, named One Eye. She*
> *lived through the barn fire.*
> ~ *Toni K. Campbell*

TONI K.: The first time I met Mary, Jim's mother, he said, Look
what followed me home, Ma. Can I keep her?

I was mortified. As I remember, Mary ignored his question.

When Jim started school, he wouldn't talk, so they sent him to
a psychiatrist. The psychiatrist asked Jim why he wouldn't talk, and
he said, I don't need to.

I mean, if you have that many brothers and sisters, they're
probably doing a lot of talking for you! So, after that he didn't have
to see the psychiatrist anymore.

Jim's responsibility on the Ashby farm was taking care of the
chickens. He had one as a special pet, named One Eye. She lived
through the barn fire.

Jim was very close to his Grandfather Campbell and enjoyed
spending time with him, and now he likes to garden like his grandfather did.

Jim and Ethan

Jim, 1982

Jim and Madison

Toni K., Jim and Ethan

CHAPTER TWENTY-ONE

Sherrill Campbell

I love Christmas at the Campbells'. There are always babies to hold and stories to be told.

~Sherrill

First of all, let me tell you that your letter caused quite a stir among the in-laws! Within hours I received calls from Roger's wife April, and Jim's wife Toni, questioning the whole favorite daughter-in-law thing. Oh, well. Sometimes the truth hurts. Ha ha!

I hardly know where to start. Twenty-three years with the Campbells is a long time!

I can remember as a little girl, my mother, who was a classmate of Mary's, telling me upon entering the church on a Sunday, Do you see that whole row of people?

After I nodded, she continued, They are all the same family!

I was quite impressed because, as you can imagine, the family took up an entire pew in the church. So, that was my first experience with the Campbells. I am still pretty impressed today.

When people ask me what we're doing for the holidays, I can honestly say I am getting together with a whole crew of people. Holidays number anywhere from 25 to 75 people!

Thirteen *is* a Lucky Number

Dave and I met while I was working at Aroostook Trust Company. I had just broken up with my high school sweetheart and Leah Ewing, a family friend of the Campbells and my boss at the bank, informed me when Dave came into the bank that I should be introduced to him, as he would treat me like a queen on a pedestal.

The next time Dave came in to cash a check, he came to my window. I thought he was so handsome (and still feel that way today). And so the relationship began. Dave was actually on his way to Texas shortly after that to spread his wings and experience a little of the world. We had a long-distance writing relationship for a couple of months, and then he came home for Christmas. Things didn't really

Sherrill and Dave

Brad, Dave, Sherrill and Daniel

go very well during that visit. My ex-boyfriend was home, too, and I was torn with who to spend time with. But eventually, I made the decision that would change my life. For the better, I might add.

Dave brought me home to meet the family. He came to get me *two hours late* but did have a good excuse. Come to find out Sharon's trailer had burned! All of her five children paraded into Grammy's and, as you can imagine, were excited, telling about the fire, and how they had to run to Grammy's in their bare feet in the snow. It was so sad.

A new person would walk by us sitting on the couch, and Dave would say, That's my sister so-and-so, and that's my other sister so-and-so.

Thank God there wasn't a test! During this time Mary wasn't very fond of me but now, I am the favorite! I think she was afraid that I wasn't quite right for Mommy's Boy. Ha ha.

After Christmas break, Dave went back to Texas, and I was working and had my own apartment.

In February, Dave's grandfather died, bringing him home to The County for good. From then on we were pretty inseparable.

We were married on July 29, 1983. It was a beautiful wedding. We pretty much tried to incorporate all the family in one way or another. I sang "Endless Love" to Dave, and still feel the sentiment of that song so much today.

We had Daniel Allen Campbell on October 15, 1985. He was the first grandchild with the Campbell name. We are pretty proud of that! Bradley Adam came along 20 months later on June 19, 1987. He was every bit the opposite of his brother but loved just as much.

I can hardly believe that the boys are grown and leaving the nest. Dan is a junior next year at Saint Joseph's College of Maine, and Brad will attend there too, as a freshman. I am not so sure what I will do with the whole empty nest thing. I was pretty much an anal mother. You would think that with as many children as Mary had, it would have been easy with all of the advice she offered, but I must say she never meddled with my raising of the boys. She was always there to answer any questions but never said I was doing anything wrong or offered unsolicited advice. Thanks, Mary!

Life with the Campbells has always been eventful. I had a surprise birthday party for Dave when he turned 30. He had been a little depressed and I thought a party with his family and friends would be just the remedy. So, I invited about 35 people to our house (which was pretty small) to cheer him up. I had worked out arrangements for getting him to the party with my favorite outlaw, Stuart, Barb's husband. He was supposed to take him to pick up or look at a snow sled.

They stopped by The Jade Palace Tikki Lounge for one drink. Barb was working there as a waitress at the time. Well, one drink turned into another, and pretty soon they were late. Three hours later and a snowstorm that was a nor'easter with power outages, and 35 people still waiting for Dave to come in the dark in my small house to his own birthday party. I was pretty livid.

I couldn't call him though because the power was out and the Jade phone worked on electricity. Several people volunteered to go to The Jade, but Mother Mary was adamant that we all stay together. I think she was pretty sure the party at The Jade was going to be more successful than mine.

I met Stuart at the door with a flashlight and some pretty harsh words before we got the surprise in. Apparently, Dave wanted to surprise us on his birthday and not show up.

We had a house fire in 2002. That really shows who your family and friends are. We lost things, but not each other, and that's what's important. I don't know how everyone knew, but slowly, each member of the Campbell family drove up with the fire trucks still there to be sure we were okay and to see what they could do to help.

Those who came to shingle our roof in the snow will always be my heroes. Thanks, Stu. Also, Jim put many hours in removing old burned plaster walls and a chimney. The family sent us money which we took under duress (you are really humbled after a tragedy like that) and attended fund-raisers that the community held for us. Sometimes I think the organizations that put the fund-raisers on thought they were being invaded by Campbells!

Being the favorite outlaw, I think I should say that all of us (in-laws, that is) are pretty terrific. It takes a special person to be able to jump into such a large family. Although, for the most part, everyone just seems to have been part of the family forever.

Thirteen *is* a Lucky Number

Some of my fondest memories are just being together. Many summer picnics out back on the hill (some land that Robert's father owned), with the beautiful views, and then sledding down the hill in the winter on toboggans.

I love Christmas at the Campbells'. There are always babies to hold and stories to be told. And the famous summer Potato Blossom Festival gatherings. You never know who you'll run into on Fort Hill Street during that time.

Overall, I couldn't have picked a more diverse family to marry into. I can't say it has always been rosy, but we do love each other, and I am proud to carry the Campbell name.

CHAPTER TWENTY-TWO

Jenny

Gramp was harder on his family than he was on the hired help. Everyone always said if you could work for Robert, you could work for anyone.

~Jenny [Sharon's daughter]

JENNY: I'm really special. I'm the oldest grandchild. I started working for Grampy and Grammy when I was really young. I used to work at the store in Easton, so I stayed here at Grammy's and Grampy's a lot. Actually, Dad was always on the road and I didn't get along very well with all my sisters and Mom. I guess I was more of a rebel. There's one in every family. That'd be me, huh, Gramp?

I remember working at the store. Gramp kept me hard at work and he taught me a lot when I worked at the store, like how to keep the money a certain way—all going the same way in the cash register. And to this day I do the same exact thing at the bank. I break open the money and rearrange it. It was one of my pet peeves when you had to share a register with somebody. I'd say, The money has to go the exact same way.

BOB: She unloaded freight and piled it. Then we had to put it on the shelves and keep track of what we had in the back room.

JENNY: I did everything at the store. I did inventory and I

Mémère, Mary, Toni [Mary's sister], Richard [Regina's husband], Loretta

helped with bakery, made sandwiches, and worked the cash register. We stuffed newspapers. At the end I was even grinding meat. It was so disgusting at first. I remember the first couple times I did it; I thought it was so gross. I waitressed in the restaurant when Gramp didn't have any help. Waitresses are hard to come by.

Working at the store taught me a lot. It made a lot of things easier, like doing schoolwork. It helped me a lot because I was in High School DECA [Distributive Education Club of America] business program, and I placed first and second because I was physically doing a job already. I was also chosen as a state representative to the National FHA [Future Homemakers of America] Convention in Chicago.

I traveled every day after school to go to work, clear to Easton from Caribou. Quite the haul for me. It was 13 miles from Fort. I got to drive but I hated the station wagon. It burned oil really bad. The smoke came out, so we called it the Batmobile.

Mary and Bob—A liquor license for the AG store in Easton

The business in Fort Fairfield

BOB: It was good training for them to learn to work with people and know what to expect when they get out in life, what they wanted to do. Jim, Joan, and Janet worked in the store, but Jenny was the only grandchild to work there. Jessica worked just a little while.

JENNY: Gramp was harder on his family than he was on the hired help. Everyone always said if you could work for Robert, you could work for anyone.

There was one time I was supposed to open and I showed up late. Only five minutes, so I lucked out. Gramp was still great after we did something wrong. He would introduce me as his daughter, so half the people in Easton used to think I was his daughter. They see me, even today, they say, How's your father?

You mean my grandfather?

It was great to stay with Grampy and Grammy, especially in the summertime, because Janet, Joan, and Kim still lived here. I think we all had our own little place we wanted to be. I always liked to be here. I used to keep Gramp straight. Huh, Gramp? Tina was always at Roland's and Steffie's. Jessica got to go to her friend's house.

BOB: We had the store 10 years after we farmed for 18 years and after we won the Megabucks. We still had the sewing center. The town of Easton built the store as a finished shell. I put in the walk-in coolers, the freezer, and meat room. We put in the fixtures. It took us a month and we did it all ourselves, too.

JENNY: I helped with that, cleaning and straightening out, stocking shelves after the orders came. We had a restaurant. Grammy made curtains for that.

After we got going, we'd find out there was a need in town. Usually someone would come into the store and tell us. Mona Fuller, in the bakery, would do up the rolls, and we'd do meat and cheese platters. We did dinner boxes for needy families and delivered them.

BOB: Whenever there was a death in town, we provided the food for the gatherings afterwards. I've always been a firm believer that when you get, you give back. That's where the income came from, so it's only natural to give it back. It's no big thing. It wouldn't be more than $20. It wasn't a thing that you kept count of. It's like

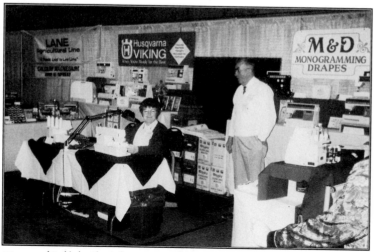

Mary and Bob's booth at the Presque Isle Forum

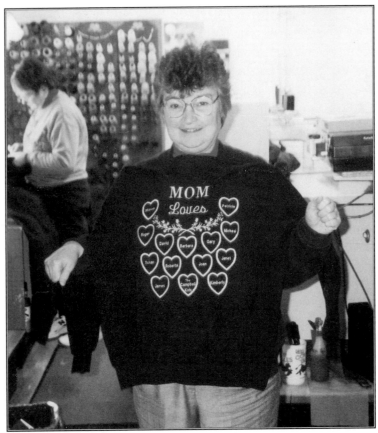

Mary Jane Clark and Mary at M&D Monogramming

counting how many times you bought groceries. Just did as we needed to. That's all. Mary made baked beans, salads, and desserts. It's nothing that we went out of our way for. We enjoyed doing it. It was natural. We were supposed to.

You don't get so busy that you can't take time to do stuff. That's one thing that I can say about us—we were never so busy, or had anything planned, that if anybody died or took sick, we couldn't go. Or anybody we had working for us. If they had somebody take sick, I don't care if it was digging and they were driving a truck—go! The work will be here just the same. Just find somebody else to put in their place.

Mary came to help out when she needed during the hours that she wasn't open [8 a.m. to 8 p.m.] at the sewing center. She didn't leave that to work at the grocery store, but she helped out on Sunday.

JENNY: Before I got my license, Grammy brought me to work at the store. We'd take a different way on back roads every time to see how many ways there were to get to Easton from Caribou. She showed me all of them.

BOB: We weren't making money, so we decided to sell the store, and it's still going. I paid too much for it in the beginning. Then the town boycotted the store. That really knocked it.

JENNY: When we started, Easton was a dry town. The town voted to sell beer. So, when we were able to sell beer, we put it in the store. No one who went to church came, especially after church. A few would still come.

BOB: I put it up for a vote in the town to put beer in the store so I could get a beer license. They didn't want to and said I was foolish to try. I said, Well, I'll try anything once.

So I tried. I had people come in and sass me about it. My idea was that they went to Presque Isle to buy their beer, and when they're over there, they buy their groceries. So, what's wrong with me selling it? I'm not asking people who don't drink to buy beer. I'm after the guys who go to Presque Isle to buy beer, and they buy their groceries there. I feel like all the systems should be treated the same. I should have the same right that Presque Isle has.

Well, they had rigged the vote. We had to run it again because the girl who worked in the town office counted the absentee ballots. She counted the "no" ballots and didn't count the "yes" ballots. She knew who would be against and who would be for. She got fired and they had another vote. It passed by a very slim margin. I was in the newspapers and everywhere.

After they voted it in, the church people boycotted me. Then we got movies in. They protested that because there were some R-movies, even though they were up and out of the way. The ones who boycotted originally were embarrassed after a while. They'd come in and buy their 12-packs.

The postmaster was the worst. He belonged to the church and a lot of people who were for it didn't get flyers on it. The year after we got that, Sunday sales were opened up to the big stores. When they did that, Smythe's moved to another location and went three times as big. They ran a sale for three months that took away from me. Right after that, Grave's Shop 'n Save went three times as big, and did the same thing. The next spring, IGA was built in Mars Hill. That took people down there.

We got killed in the meantime and started getting debt. In the beginning, the company put stock in on consignment. When we started going down, we had to pay cash. I started having $8,000 worth of stock coming in twice a week. It was hard. We'd miss a payment, they'd fine us. I lived through it.

I can't tell you the year or the day, but it was in February. The meat cutter I had was the best man I ever had work for me. He was a good man. He was very good to all the customers. He was awful good to the help, especially the women. Before he went home at night, he'd ask if there was anything we needed lifted, cleaned, or moved.

Joan caught him stealing. And we'd caught him once before, so we let him go. He knew we'd caught him when we told him, and he said he'd never do it again, but he did, so I fired him. The guy did everything but get on his knees and beg to stay.

I said to him, Can't be done. The other clerks in there, what would they think? They could just pick up everything and still have a job? I can't have that. I know you're a good man and I appreciate that. Well, he went out and got in his car and, God, he come back in about a half hour later, begged and begged. He said, I'll work for half the wages.

I said, If you worked for nothing, I couldn't have you, because it ain't fair to the other people working here.

So he said, Okay.

I had bought tickets for him to go out to the Sportsmen's supper at the VFW in Caribou that night. He went home and I went to the supper. Next morning about four o'clock, Presque Isle cops called and wanted to know if I could go over. I went over to Presque Isle police station and wanted to know what was the trouble. They said they were calling me in to find out if I knew anything about this man. I said, Yeah. He used to work for me.

50th Anniversary of Potato Blossom Festival, Blaine House, 1997
Mildred Bennett and Mary

They asked, How long has he been done?

Last night. I fired him last night. Why? Did he get himself in some trouble?

The policeman said, Well, he shot his wife and himself. The boy came home and found them.

That was too bad. So, that sickened me of the store, really. Right then. He could have come back in, shot some people in the store just as well as not.

We saw hardships. There were families who had worked hard, hard all their lives. They'd get $12 for food stamps and the government would cut them down to $8. Then, there were young people going on Skidoos and they'd come in with $100 or $150 worth of food stamps, and the other poor people couldn't get any more than that.

JENNY: There was a man who went psycho on me one day. I said, Have a good day.

He said, You expect me to have a good day?

Gramp came out of the office that day.

You expect me to have a good day? I could go outside, fall on my head and split it open.

On and on about what could happen to him.

He'd say to Gramp, I could shoot you just as well as not.

He was a dairy farmer from New Hampshire. He was awful. After he passed away, it was really sad because their kids were so much more relaxed when they came in. They'd even say hi. The police were afraid of him. If he thought they were coming, he was ready for them. He'd get the water hose and turn it on them when they got to his house. They could never get him when he did anything wrong. He'd say they shouldn't be on his property. He never did hurt anybody, but everybody was scared of him. Mary was scared to death of him.

MARY: I had been to church on Saturday night. When Megabucks got to a big amount, they'd be quite busy at the store, so I went to help the girls.

He said, You ought to be in the morgue. You're dressed up for the morgue.

He'd say weird things to you.

BOB: There was a guy with a mustache. He came in. He knew everything about everything. He'd argue about everything and he was loud. When I say loud, I mean loud, and he'd make sure that everyone heard him.

I don't give a goddamn if you like me or not, this is the way it is.

On and on. He was a good customer but he'd drive the others crazy. They'd get their stuff and go, and he'd still be in there raving.

JENNY: It was a good time to go to the bathroom. Gramp would come and run the cash register.

MARY: We had a couple of break-ins at the store. One time, they left the tire iron that they used right in the store. Someone set fire to the trash can.

BOB: One time it burned inside, too. The insurance paid but they had three deductibles: $1,000 on the outside, $1,000 on the inside, and $1,000 on the contents. I lost $3,000 right there. Plus you don't get everything out of the insurance company. They just pay you for what it cost at the place. They don't add freight on, interest, or handling.

CHAPTER TWENTY-THREE

Letters from the Grandchildren

October 2005

Dear Grammy and Grampy,

I have a lot of good memories of going to your house even though I'm only five years old.

Usually when I go over to your house there are other kids to play with and we like to run around and play upstairs.

I also like going out on the porch to color and draw pictures. And when I was little I used to like playing with the beads you have.

In July, during the Potato Blossom Festival, I like going over to play with everyone and watch the fireworks in the backyard.

I also remember and liked it when Dad, Mom, Alan, and I went to Island Falls. I had a lot of fun. I did a lot of swimming, even after I jumped in the deep end, and Alan and Dad had to rescue me.

I like being in the Campbell family because we have a lot of fun, no matter where we all meet.

Love ya,
Amanda

Grammy and Grampy,

I think I could write a book about how proud I am to have the two of you as my grandparents but I'm going to keep it simple. Grampy, I want to thank you for giving me your stubbornness and will to never give up on the things that matter the most to me. Grammy, I want to thank you for your quiet heart and undying love for each and every one of us. But most of all, I want to thank the two of you for teaching me that I am as rich as gold, not because of what is in my bank account, but because I have a family that is filled with love and happiness.

Happy 50th Anniversary!! I love you, Janelle Zeigler

Nicole, Jonathan, Christopher, Kayla, Saré

September 18, 2005

I like to go to Island Falls with Grammy and Grampy
because we go swimming.
I like to play store at their house.
It is fun.
Kayla Giberson

Nicole, Christopher and Kayla

Thirteen *is* a Lucky Number

September 18, 2005

Dear Grammy & Grampy,

I like to play with Grampy's tractors when I go to your house.
Thank you for letting me ride on your scooter, Grampy.

I like your house because it is so big. I like going to Island Falls
with you in the summer. I love swimming. You are great grandparents.

I love you.

Chris Giberson

—⟫◆⟪—

Dear Grammy and Grampy,

Grammy, I'm looking forward to learning to sew with you.
I know you are looking forward to teaching me.

Oh, and thank you for cooking all those delicious meals at
Island Falls.

I love you lots,

Nicole

CHAPTER TWENTY-FOUR

Loretta Decker

We all sat at a big long table with mounds of food, especially potatoes. Bob told us, Company is served first, but take all you want to eat because there will be no seconds.

~Loretta, Mary's sister

I lived away, but when we went to visit Mom and Dad, Mary always had us for dinner and, of course, with farming, that was at noon. I was amazed at the number of children she had. We all sat at a big long table with mounds of food, especially potatoes. Bob would tell us, Company is served first, but take all you want to eat because there will be no seconds.

Of course, it took forever to get dishes done.

My children loved going there to play on a farm.

When I visited Caribou, people would tell us what a remarkable family the Campbells were in church—all lined up, clean, and hair braided or long. The boys were always spiffy, too. Mr. Nadeau the town barber always made this a big story to tell us.

After farming and then starting the sewing machine business, Mary and a friend booked a tour to Europe. I was in Germany at the time and they were coming to spend a week with us. We went to Frankfort airport, and no Mary, so we had to wait for the next plane

Thirteen *is* a Lucky Number

from Spain to come in. I was a wreck and so worried. Here she comes on the second plane, all alone. We found out she had taken the tour alone. Now, that's a brave girl from northern Maine. Our German landlady was with us and couldn't believe it. Our German and American friends loved her and were so impressed. She came home with lots of wine.

Mary and Bob also bought Mom and Dad tickets to come visit us in Germany for two weeks. It was great.

They were always so generous to both sets of parents.

They also furnished potatoes and turnips to the Holy Rosary School lunch.

When Mary went to the hospital to have Barb, and then Dave, I stayed with the older children. I was busy all day and at least 'til two a.m. to keep her home like she left it. The drawers full of tiny folded baby clothes were all so neat. Plus, Bob had to have donuts and fresh bread every day, but his Mom made those and they were delicious. Bob also loved cookies, but the ones I made were too small. He wanted cookies the size of a plate, so his Mom took over that task, too.

For sure, Mary is a great mother, wife, sister, and everything else. I look at her as a matriarch and a saint.

Chapter Twenty-Five

Antoinette (Toni) Phillips

*The Hudson Bay blanket, draped over the front seat, looked
like an invitation for Carolyn Duncan and I to hide in the
backseat.*

~ Toni, Mary's sister

Toni: Mary, my mind has been on overload with all the memories. My question is, Where do I start? Here are some memory sparks.

⟫◆⟪

You and I were partners in a booby trap. We pushed the chest of drawers to the top of the stairs, trying to trap Loretta and Regina downstairs. We got it too close to the edge and it crashed down one flight of stairs. Luckily, Mom was working at Birds Eye that night and Dad wasn't too hard on us. Soft touch, Dad.

⟫◆⟪

Remember all the fun we had picking potatoes at Percy and Wayne Buck's farm? You had such a crush on Wayne and how we laughed at you when he spoke to you, and you blushed so, that your face looked like a lit-up Christmas wreath.

———◆———

Sam's was our second home from May through September. Remember all the D2 fights and all the boy-surfing we did?

———◆———

When you and Bob were dating, he came to pick you up to go to the Polaris Drive-in in his 1949 Hudson. The Hudson Bay blanket, draped over the front seat, looked like an invitation for Carolyn Duncan and I to hide in the backseat. Yes, we made it through the ticket booth, and to this day, I can't figure out how Carolyn and I stifled our giggles for so long.

Surprise! Please tell me why you didn't see any humor that night?

The pranks stopped when I was all ready for a night out with my friends, when Bob shoved my head under the kitchen faucet and turned the water on. I had very thick, long hair at the time, and it was before blow-dryers were invented. Yes, it was payback!

———◆———

I remember going to the Ashby farm for Christmas dinner in 1970. Michele was two years old and Curtis was six. What a day they had with all their cousins. Michele was under the table in her hand-smocked red dress and white tights, chasing the cat and crawling over lots of little feet, with Uncle Bob saying, A little dirt won't hurt her.

Celebration of Life party for Mémère, May 30, 2004

⟫◆⟪

I went out to the farm to babysit while you drove Mrs. Campbell down to Waterville to a foot specialist. I had Kim, Janet, and Joan, along with my two, Curtis and Michele. Then, the school bus came. I was asking myself, what do I do now? We managed getting through supper and it was time to get ready for bed. I stood in the laundry room scratching my head and wondered, How do you do this, Mary? You do this every day.

⟫◆⟪

It was 1991 and Dad was very ill and at Cary Medical Center. The four of us were home to see him. After a long day and evening, we four sisters stayed at the Caribou Motor Inn. Regina and Toni introduced you and Loretta to Grand Marnier. Dad's Golden Girls were having too much fun when the front desk called to inform us that they had a complaint from newlyweds who were in the next

Forty pink balloons for Mémère, May 30, 2004

room. Some people just have no sense of humor. You trained us well, Dad!

—————◆—————

One of the happiest days of Mom's life was her 80th birthday, December 27, 1999. Bob O'Brien wanted the four Golden Girls and Mom at our house at 11 a.m. We watched Mom's mouth drop when we went to the front door and saw a shiny, black stretch limo back up into the driveway. Bob planned everything! We were off to the Ritz-Carlton in Boston for Sunday brunch.

What a wonderful day we had! Our driver couldn't believe that we were sisters and were having so much fun, let alone the fact that our mother was with us. Mom talked about this day until God came to take her.

—————◆—————

It was February 11, 2001, when we learned that Mom had to go to a nursing home. The four of us had to close up her apartment.

After a very stressful day, we spent the night at our Fort Fairfield house. We got into our pj's and sat around the master bedroom, with the full moon and bright stars lighting the room. Our shared stories were mixed with laughter and tears, and we found out that we all had a little of Mom in us.

Thank you, Sharon, Terry, Roger, and Barbara for helping us that sad day.

———⇒◆⇐———

It was January 24, 2004, at Presque Isle Nursing Home. After reciting a decade of the rosary with Mom just a few hours before she went to meet Dad, she looked at each of us and said, I have my four shining stars.

We replied, We have our angel.

Mary, there is no doubt in my mind that you were the brightest star in Mom's eyes that night. Yes, you are the matriarch of our family now, and I don't know anyone who has worked any harder to earn that title. We love you.

~Toni

CHAPTER TWENTY-SIX

13 Nieces and Nephews

The Campbell Girls

TONI: We could not have picked a better title for the Campbell story.

Thirteen is a Lucky Number! can be interpreted in so many ways—13 different personalities, careers, and now, each of your own families. You are all so very special in your individual ways.

It never ceased to amaze everyone how well-behaved thirteen children could be, whether you were at Mud Lake or in someone's home. You all knew what was expected of you, and the big kids watched the little ones.

Knowing some of you better than others, I'm wondering how you all grew up so fast. I distinctly remember your school days, weddings, and now, I'm watching most of you as parents, and yes, some of you as grandparents.

Sharon, it was an eye-opener watching you at Lori and Randy's wedding reception, seeing that everything was running smoothly, looking beautiful, and confident as the true matriach of your family.

Pat, it is always so nice to see you, Wayne, and sometimes your children giving so much of your time to the community. Be certain it doesn't go unnoticed.

Barbara, my godchild, a wonderful mother and grandmother, you will always have a special spot in my heart. After hearing some of your childhood stories, we are all so fortunate that you had so many guardian angels.

Joan, I still see that beautiful bride having so much fun at her wedding reception, getting everyone out on the dance floor. Yes, Sean, you were going around pinching butts.

Sue, I remember the summer of 1994 when I was hostess at the Gull Inn for the summer, and you helped clean a few of the rooms. I never had to clean behind you. It was always done to perfection.

Roberta, dunk it! No one will ever forget that basketball tournament when you helped Fort Tigers bring home that trophy. You are so good at everything you do—wife, mother, career, and very quick at putting up the CAUTION WET FLOOR sign when needed.

Janet, you are known around town as the incredible mailman, delivering mail on your route with one hand, and lending a helping hand with the other. When your name is mentioned around Fort Fairfield, I am very proud to tell them that you are my niece.

Kim, with your ever-ready blushing smile, you are now a wife, mother, and more beautiful than ever.

The Campbell Boys

Roger, David, Gary, Mike, and Jim, you all have come a long way since the boxing glove days, and you survived. Luckily, you outsmarted your sisters.

Roger, although I haven't seen you for a while, I close my eyes and see that little boy in that BIG body. After looking at the pictures of the Celebration of Life Reunion we had in honor of Grammie Guerrette, I see you happily sharing your stories with your cousins, and being the BIGGEST kid, playing games with all the little ones.

David, Gary, and Jim, I'm certain that you know how special it is for me to be back in The County and getting reacquainted with you and your families.

Mike, with your gentle mannerisms and smile, I hope to see a lot more of you in 2006.

You boys have grown up to be wonderful and handsome young men. Yeah, you too, Roger.

To all of you, when you feel you have a big, black cloud hanging over your heads, remember Grammie's party, when after 39 pink balloons out of 40 were launched to heaven (with four-year-old Daniel hanging on to his for dear life because he thought Mémère had enough), the sun broke through that huge black cloud on that memorable day. Yes, Grammie Guerrette, our angel, will smile down on you like she did on all of us who were there that day.

The year 2006 will be a very special one, starting with your parents' 50th wedding anniversary on the 6th of February, Sharon turning 50, your mom's 50th Class Reunion, and the first book signing of the Campbell story.

Yes, you are definitely worth writing about. A treasure to be passed down from one generation to the next.

May God protect and bless all of you, and always know how much you are loved.

~Auntie

⟹•◇•⟸

Thank you, Bob O'Brien, for making this happen, and letting people know what this wonderful family is all about.

—◆—

Trudy Chambers Price, author and now a very special friend to our family, many thanks for your long hours of recording and endless disciplined effort to write this story.

~Toni

CHAPTER TWENTY-SEVEN

Regina Anderson

The pig had a name, I think. Then the pig went for slaughter.
I always wondered how the kids could eat their own pet. But
that's farm life, I guess.
~Regina, Mary's sister

When Sharon was born in 1956, I was 11 years old. I remember going to Litchfield, Connecticut, with Mom and Dad to visit them. Sharon was the sweetest baby in the world.

By the time Patricia was born in 1957, Mary and Bob had moved back to Maine. Yet another beautiful baby was welcomed into the family. And so it went for 13 years.

When Mary and Bob first came back to Maine, they lived in a small farmhouse behind Mr. and Mrs. Campbell's, John and Elizabeth. Every year, Mary had a beautiful vegetable garden. And she made her own bread and dinner rolls, as Robert's upbringing had accustomed him to that. And she worked alongside Bob on the farm, especially during harvest.

The young girls, Sharon, Pat, and Barbara, baked beautiful cakes.

I remember the boys sleeping up in the loft of the little farmhouse and raising the devil. Bob would go up there and lay the law down and it became somewhat quiet.

Richard [Regina's husband] and Mary

When I was home for summer vacation, I remember going out to the farm and having to visit the kids' pet pigs. One of them came to the fence and planted a kiss on one of the kids' faces. They dared me to do the same but I couldn't do it. The pig had a name, I think. Then the pet pig went to slaughter. I always wondered how the kids could eat their own pet. But that's farm life, I guess.

They had a pony at one time, which they wanted me to ride. I got up on the pony and immediately fell to the ground on my butt. Everyone laughed. I wish I had gone back onto the pony's back, because to this day I still have a fear of horses.

And then there was the family pet cow. She was named Sun Van Della. At one of Bob and Mary's barn dances that Richard and I attended, someone brought the cow onto the dance floor to Richard. It had a sign stuck to its horn saying, DICK'S LOVE. What fun we had that night. That was before the fire that demolished their barn.

Our mother always worked for Bob and Mary during potato harvest. One time I asked Mom why she brought tuna fish for lunch every day. She said that one of Mary's girls (I think it was Sue or Janet) loved tuna and would trade lunch with her Grammie every day.

CHAPTER TWENTY-EIGHT

Doris Chamberlain

Bob said, Mary, better go look. There's one somewhere not being fed.

~*Doris Haley Chamberlain, Bob's cousin*

When we lived on the Sealander Road on what we called the Sealander Farm for 26 years, our daughter Ann had a little palomino mare named Honey. She was just big enough to be in a horse class.

Every time Bob and Mary would come visit, the children would be taken with that horse because she was so trustworthy. It's like she enjoyed them more than they enjoyed her. She just loved giving kids rides. The kids always wanted rides on Honey. We'd put the saddle on and two or three of them would pile on. Some of them would be following along on the side just waiting for their turns to have a ride. Sometimes they'd get to bumping along and someone would slide off the back.

I remember one particular time giving them rides, and kids were on the horse's back and we were going along very slowly, but the grass happened to be wet. One of them, I don't remember which one, came running head-on toward the horse. She had clover or something for Honey. Lo and behold, she slipped and fell right there but the horse just stopped and looked, and waited and went on. She was such a nice animal and the kids enjoyed her so much.

Mary's mother and dad had a camp at Mud Lake and they used to stop on the way, and we all looked forward to that, Ann especially, because she was alone and she loved to have them play with her.

Ernest liked horses and always had horses and I did, too. He had a stallion that was made into a gelding. Barb liked horses. The horse was pretty well-trained, so he let Barb take the horse to ride and use when they lived on the Ashby farm.

Unfortunately, the barn burned, along with the horse. But it was a horse. It was an animal. It was a really bad night—a bad storm. We were at home and the phone rang, and it was Bob. He was obviously excited. He said, I have to tell you, and I want you to know that I tried hard to get the horse out of the barn, but I couldn't get it out. The barn was burning.

I said, That's okay, Bob, don't worry about the horse. What about Mary and the kids? And how is everyone else?

Oh, he said, they're okay, they're fine.

I'm glad everybody's okay and the house is okay.

But Barb liked the horse so much, we felt badly. I always thought that with everything going on that Bob would stop to call us about that. It says what kind of person he is.

Mary had invited us out to supper at the Ashby farm. The Ashbys were related to me. Mrs. Ashby was my dad's sister. Small world. That was a large house, and in the kitchen there was a picnic table–type thing with a tablecloth. The kids used to sit there on benches and there was a dining room.

Mary was so smart, always so smart. She'd make pies and, not like me, I'd slap the cover on the top. But she'd lace them all, basket-weave crust, and everything was so nice. Mary had all that cooking to do, all that work to do, and she took the time and patience to do something extra.

So finally, everyone settled down to eat, and there was the regular commotion of people getting ready to have their meal. All of a sudden, there was a little child that kind of whimpered, made a noise, made known that they were there.

Bob said, Mary, better go look. There's one somewhere not being fed.

She went to take a look out in the kitchen where the kids were eating. She came back and she was laughing. She said, Yes, it was the little one, Kim, in the high chair by the refrigerator, where no one was paying attention. Now, we can eat.

They lived in the little house at the Campbell farm on the East Presque Isle Road. Mary was very good to Bob's parents, John and Lizzie.

After my father [Leo Haley] died, my mother and we were all there at the funeral home. John was elderly and not too well. Two of the boys brought him to the funeral home. John said to Robert's two boys, You boys can go now. You don't need to be here. You can go downtown and can do anything you want. After hours, you can come back and pick me up.

One of the boys said, No, Grampy, Dad told us to stay here with you today, and so we're staying.

And they did. They stayed there. I thought, boy, they really respect their father and know when he asks or tells them what they should do. They followed through even though the grandfather had told them they were excused.

Robert tells the story about during harvest in the fall when they lived on the Ashby farm. He was up early, early in the morning. One of the older girls was the only one up with him. They always bought those huge boxes of dry cereal and he said he was going to have dry cereal. So, he went in the pantry and got the cereal and put it in his bowl. He was kind of sleepy, you know, when you're up early, early in the fall of the year and your eyes are half sleepy. He took the milk and put it on his cereal. She was doing something in the kitchen. Bob said, What are all these things floating on the milk in my cereal?

She went over and took a look. Well, she said, one of the kids spilled that big box of corn flakes on the floor yesterday. I knew we couldn't waste that, so I swept it up and put it back in the box.

Oh, that's what it is.

When we were kids we used to go to the East Presque Isle Road to visit. Our uncle and aunt Freeland and Annie Smith lived on that farm. The next farm is where Uncle John and Aunt Kate Haley lived. The next farm was John and Lizzie Campbell's who are relatives as well. Skip just one farm where the Gilmans lived. Then the McGlinns lived on the next farm, so when we went out to visit, we were there for a few days visiting. I was about nine or ten, old enough to stay away from home and be lonesome and cry a little bit. My brother Burnham and my sister Leola were older, but Gwen and I would stay all night, and some of the others would come and stay all night. We'd be at one house but we'd visit with the others. Usually we'd get lonesome. I was probably the one who'd get lonesome more than anyone else, and we'd have to go home. Don Smith would come out and visit. We went camping—real camping—with the Smiths and Haleys down to Connecticut and over to Canada.

John used to have a picnic once a year at the campground down by the stream. He roasted corn and all the relatives would gather there.

CHAPTER TWENTY-NINE

Ralph Gallagher

*Before my wife and I were married, I suggested we go over to visit
Robert and Mary one evening. With my future wife sitting on
the sofa, each and every one of them paraded by to inspect her.*
　　~Ralph

My name is Ralph Gallagher, and I am a first cousin of
Robert's. There are a lot of things that I could say about Robert, but
I'll only make a few remarks that include his whole family.

I used to go visit them when I, along with them, was a lot
younger. Many times I'd go over on my 50cc motorbike. Believe you
me, sometimes it would be nearly an hour before I could get into the
house to visit. There were, perhaps only about 10 of them then, that
would be lined right up waiting for a ride.

Before my wife and I were married, I suggested we go over to
visit Robert and Mary one evening. With my future wife sitting on
the sofa, each and every one of them paraded by to inspect her. I
guess that she passed inspection with all of them because there was
no bad feedback. That was perhaps about 32 years ago.

At about this same time, they used to sponsor a barn dance in
the big barn that was on the Ashby farm where they lived and
farmed. Neighbors, family, friends, and even people that they didn't

know, would show up for an evening of wonderful entertainment and fun. There would be a live band and plenty of food and drink for everyone. That all came to an end when the huge barn burned on Groundhog Day in 1976. They were great fun and a wonderful memory.

CHAPTER THIRTY

Amy McGlinn

As far as I'm concerned, I don't think there's a better person in this world than Mary.
~Amy McGlinn

I was married to Nason McGlinn. He and Rob were first cousins on his mother's side of the family. Nason's father and Rob's mother were brother and sister. Nason's father was the only man in the family. There were four girls and one boy. Nason was more Roland's age and they used to do a lot together, like go to the basketball tournaments down to Bangor. That was the big deal back then.

I liked Rob's mother Lizzie. She was very down-to-earth. And she spoke her mind. And Rob is *very* outspoken.

Rob was younger, and I remember one of the first social events we went to with him and Mary. They were so busy having their children and taking care of them that they didn't get to go out that much until the children had grown some. We went to Pete's Maple Grove with them and had a great time.

As far as I'm concerned, I don't think there's a better person in this world than Mary. All through, she's accepted having the family she's had. She's been a wonderful mother to them all, and she still is. They have a lovely family. Rob and Mary are my son Darrin's godparents.

Thirteen *is* a Lucky Number

Before we were married and were going together, Nason was working for John McHugh. Nason was working in the potato house. The potato storage bin let go, the potatoes poured out, and Nason was buried up to his neck in potatoes. The more they tried to get him out, the more potatoes would keep rolling down on him. By the time they got him out, they had to take him to the hospital. He wasn't physically injured but he was kind of in shock.

This was on a Saturday. I was working at Sears & Roebuck at the time. A friend of his came in to say that Nason wasn't going to be there for our date because he was in the hospital. I didn't believe his friend because I thought they wanted to do something that night, and that was the excuse, which wasn't very smart of me because they wouldn't do something serious like that. So, I walked down to the drugstore after work and John McHugh was sitting on a stool, having a soda. I looked at him and said, Is that true?

He said, Yuh, he was buried for quite a while.

They let him out the next day.

After Nason's mother asked him to come back to run the farm, he also did shift work for Maine Public Service for 41 years. All our kids worked, but our son Andy was the one who loved to farm, so he stayed here.

We lived here on the farm with Nason's mother for 18 years and never had a cross word between us. She was such a wonderful person. She loved to talk farm and she was determined to keep the farm. The home place has 60 acres. John Skonieczny bought Carl Rasmussen's farm [Ned Townsend's at the time]. Andy worked for John before he bought John out. Andy rents other farms, too.

Speaking of the picnic area on the hill of the Campbell Farm, my grandson, Kirk Fongemie, was married on that hill last summer. He married Jennifer Micoleau. His mother is my daughter Jackie from Alaska. It was the most gorgeous day and the most wonderful wedding. It couldn't have been better. Kirk's aunt Carol did the catering. Kirk's family moved to Alaska when he was a junior in high school, but he came back and spent his senior year here with us. He adores Uncle Andy and they've always had a good relationship. This is where he wanted to be married, and Jen agreed to it.

When we had the McGlinn reunion in 2004, Mary and all of her children worked on it. There were close to 200 who came. We met every month at one place or another to plan it. That was fun, and we've been going out to eat once a month ever since.

Part III
Friends

CHAPTER THIRTY-ONE

Jeannette Peters

Kids aren't brought up like that anymore.
~*Jeannette Peters*

There were three girls on the Fort Fairfield basketball team at a time. First Bert, Joan, and Janet. Bert graduated and Kim came on as a freshman to play with Joan and Janet. Kim was a freshman starter because of her height.

They all played soccer and some of them played field hockey. In the play-off soccer game Bert was injured and was on crutches.

They all were very talented and pleasant young ladies, very nice looking, well mannered.

I have nothing but compliments for that family. It's a wonderful family. The girls are the ones I know. I knew a couple of the boys, but I knew the girls real well because they played sports for me, and they were always around me.

I can remember when Joan got hurt and I took her down to the emergency room. Back then I could take the kids and go with them and the parents agreed with it. The parking lot at the high school was just glare ice. We came back and I put my brakes on to stop. We didn't stop. We hit the school. We both sat there in the car and just laughed.

It's just times like this that those kids were so special to me. They are to this day. Joan was very quiet. She is a doll.

I see Janet and Joan all the time. I saw Kim, too. She has a new baby. It's still the same thing. It's still always, Mrs. Peters or Mrs. P. They are just wonderful, wonderful kids.

They were so much fun on the trips down east. Ken was driving a van and had another gentleman who was supposed to go, and then couldn't go because he had been kicked by a horse the night before. So, we took the Campbells' van.

When we went down east we went camping. Ken would stay with his mother because he was from Eastport. He'd come and cook breakfast or lunch for us. We had so much fun.

One time we stayed in a motel and the shower broke and those two clowns (one of them was a Campbell girl) came in, laughing their heads off. It was flooding.

We went on whale watches, something educational, but still had fun doing those things. You didn't have to worry about the little things that you have to worry about now with the parents. The kids were so good. Little things satisfied them and they had fun doing them, like just going for a walk around the beach. We took the trip every summer, and it was great for them.

In the summer we played softball, too, and Ken drove the bus. We got into some messes with those, too. We ran out of gas one time and we were playing in a tournament. A couple cars came by, we loaded the kids up and away we went. They went back and got the bus later. We wouldn't be allowed to do that now.

There have been big changes. Back then the parents would back you if you disciplined a kid. Now you don't discipline a kid because it's going to be your fault. Times have changed, big time.

I've just gotten to know Sharon, one of the older Campbell girls, at Curves where I just started working part-time. She told me about her father recently. She was at work and her father called and he said, Sharon, can you come over here at noontime?

She says, Yeah, I can, Dad.

When she got there, she found out that he had gone downtown, fallen and lost his glasses. So, he had to get Sharon and show her where to find his glasses. He'd get into messes downtown and call one of the kids to come and get him.

Look at the Campbell kids—most of them are right around here, except for four of them.

Janet's just a great, great, wonderful, girl—out-going and full of the devil. Her kids are so special to her and she's got them involved with everything she can get them involved with.

Class C Eastern Maine Softball Tournament Champions, 1988
b: Coach Jeannette Peters, manager Meg McLaughlin, manager Linda Langley, manager Kim Conant, Wendy Voisine, Stephanie Fields, Robyn Roope, Peggy Tilley, Pat Nelson, Julie Jones, Laurie Saucier, Lynn Saucier, Ken Peters
f: Jody Doody, Wendy Ames, Tina Willette, Lisa McGillan, Tina Greenier, Kim Campbell, Saré Bernier, Janelle Cote

Thirteen *is* a Lucky Number

Kim is part of Janet and Joan. I just met Kim's husband recently. They protect each other like you won't believe about anything that has happened that very few people might know about. It stays there. It's not something that's broadcast around. They're very family oriented and what happens in that family has stayed in that family. I'm sure there are some things you'll never find out about because that's how they are.

Michael's the one I know. I also had Mary [Nightingale] in school. I had Jim and Sean in school.

I knew Susan very well and the man she was married to, Chester Cyr. The Cyr family was a big family, too. Susan was shorter, with dark hair.

I know David. I know Barb, too, and Pat, but not as well.

Jessica is a beautiful girl. She's very close to a girl named Dallas that I call my daughter. I used to call all the Campbell girls my daughters.

Mary and Bob are well known around town. It's been a great family to have. To raise 13 kids has got to be unbelievable. It's not just luck. It's the way they brought them up, and I think that's what has changed in this day and age. Kids aren't brought up like that anymore.

CHAPTER THIRTY-TWO

Rodney Doody

*When I received a bid from Bob Campbell, I asked Bob, What
in the world do you want a school bus for?*
~Rodney Doody

I worked in the Fort Fairfield school system for 33 years, both
as principal and superintendent.

At a recent Rotary Club function and supper, Bob, Mary, and I
reminisced about a school bus.

From time to time the school bus fleet was rotated. As new buses
were brought into the fleet, older ones were put up for sale by bid.

Most bidders were farmers who wanted a bus to transport children to and from the potato fields during the hand-picking harvest
days of the past. Other farmers bought the older buses for parts,
since the International bus parts matched their International farm
trucks.

When I received a bid from Bob Campbell, I asked Bob, What
in the world do you want a school bus for?

Bob said, I want a bus for hauling my children and grandchildren around.

Unfortunately (fortunately in the eyes of some of the children),
Bob lost the bid.

Thirteen *is* a Lucky Number

While I was principal at Fort Fairfield High School, I got to know some of the younger Campbell children. They all had some common character traits. They had a strong work ethic, in and out of school.

All of the Campbell children that I knew were ladies and gentlemen. It was obvious to me that they had been taught by their parents to respect other people.

Some of the Campbell children were of the same ages as my own children and there were friends among them.

With so many in one family, I felt it was unusual for 13 to get along.

CHAPTER THIRTY-THREE

Arthur Benner

A barrel of potatoes weighs 165 pounds and she's rolling that like it's nothing.
    ~Arthur Benner

I worked for the Campbell family during the potato harvest break. I was a teacher at the time, so we had what's called harvest break. I worked out there for five seasons, from 1970 to 1975. They are a great family to work for. Very family oriented. They wanted good workers, and so apparently my friends and I ended up being that because we worked there for a number of years.

When we first met the Campbell family, of course, there were quite a few in the family—13 children. They always invited me to set down and eat with them at the dinner table, especially if we were working nights.

One night we set down and Mary said to me, Now, Art, make sure when the loaf of bread goes around that you take your piece because it won't be going around again.

I didn't understand what she meant, but we passed it around and there were 16 people and 16 slices. Of course, with all those people, when it ended up at her plate, she just took the package,

Mary wins the potato-picking contest, July 2000

crumpled it up, and threw it in the garbage. I was thoroughly impressed that the bread loaf made it just one time around.

We worked at the Ashby farm. Originally I was driving a bulk truck for them. Then I ended up driving the harvester.

I was working the bulk truck and was backing the truck into the barn. And sometimes the dirt wears away from the concrete. When it hit that concrete with that heavy load—all of a sudden—BANG. It broke the transmission. I thought, oh, my God almighty, he's going to fire me for sure. So, I thought, Holy gosh, now I'm going to have to pay for this. That'll be my harvest money for the fall.

Bob said, Oh, no no no, you're not going to pay for this. That could have happened to anybody. You were coming back fine. The tires just hit incorrectly, that's all. It's not your fault.

I said, I won't be working the harvest if I don't have a truck.

Bob said, Oh, yes, you'll be working. You're going to drive the harvester.

He had been kidding with me on the tractor while we were waiting for a bulk truck. He said, I know that you know what's going on and I trust you to do it.

I said, Boy, that's a big responsibility.

You can do it. I know you can.

I started driving the harvester and he worked in the potato house after he fixed that truck. Bob always drove the harvester before that. He rode with me the first couple of loads and then I was on my own. I did that for a couple of years for him. After I got through the first couple of days, I did pretty well.

You have to dig differently for russet potatoes than you do for the round whites. After a while it got to be a contest. I knew that Bob was a real good harvester. He had a Champion Harvester.

Bob moved around quite quickly. He didn't waste much time going from point A to point B. He was always laughing and joking. That's what made working the harvester with them good.

We'd dig during the day and we'd also dig at night. I've seen days that we put a lot of loads into the trucks, so my goal was to beat his record. One day we dug 18 bulk bodies full of potatoes. It was a long day but we did that. I said, Bob, I think I may have beat your record.

Mary laughed and said, You were pretty darn close. You got 18. The most Bob's ever done is 19.

I never broke the record. That just happened to be a real good day of digging. The rows were opening up just right. Everything was going fine. We didn't have many breakdowns.

Bob was always an even-tempered guy. I don't think I ever saw him angry—not once all the years I worked for him. It was quite an experience working there. I look back very fondly at those years working the harvester with Bob and Mary.

I learned a lot out there; obviously, the value of hard work. We all learn that. I learned it at an early age, but working the harvest made it stick in my mind even more, that's for sure.

The last time I saw Bob, over a year ago, I told him about the first season I worked for him. We were just married and built a house in 1970 and moved in. We had no furniture, nothing. We figured, that's okay; we've got a house. I worked all harvest and I saved all my money. I didn't spend one nickel of it and I bought a brand new La-Z-Boy chair for our living room. I told Bob that I still have that chair. In fact, I'm looking at it right now. I refinished it myself and had it reupholstered. It looks just as good as the day I bought it. I'll bet there aren't many people who still have the chair they bought back in 1970 from working on the harvest. That chair has a lot of good memories. That was a lot of hard work for that chair.

Aroostook potato field

I enjoyed a great, great family. Some of their children went to the Caribou schools. I was principal in Caribou as well as the superintendent of schools, so I know all of their children.

Bob and I always chat every time we see each other. I go to the Fort Fairfield Rotary Club to visit and I used to see him there.

Of course, they won the Megabucks. I couldn't help but think that it couldn't have happened to two nicer people. It wasn't a great big amount, but it was nice. It was good because I think they took a trip. That was great. They needed that. They've worked hard all their lives and didn't have a chance to do an awful lot because they farmed. I think everybody was happy for them, thinking that they were hardworking people and had a big family.

Yet in spite of the big family, they got along well. The kids were well mannered and polite. They all helped each other.

317

Thirteen *is* a Lucky Number

I remember Bob saying one of the funny things that they used to do was take the kids out to McDonald's once in a while. They had two vehicles. They'd go up and place an order for 14 or 15 things. That kept them busy inside McDonald's. That was quite an order.

I'm from the southern part of Maine where three or four was a big family. The Campbell kids all pitched in on everything. They all had a job and it was expected they would do their job, and they did. Typical kids, they might complain a little bit until Mary looked at them and that would be the end of that discussion.

Or there might be the typical fights between the boys and girls but nothing too serious. That's understandable growing up. When one would get into an argument, there would be two or three others who would take sides. So it would be more of a debate than a fight.

The thing that amazed me was their laundry room. When I say laundry room, they had *a laundry room!* They had one room in the house where the washer and dryer were. Oh, naturally, I mean, there were clothes everywhere in piles because all of these kids and Mary and Bob had a lot of clothes they'd go through, especially during harvest. You open that door and go into that room and there were stacks of pants, stacks of shirts, stacks of shorts, stacks of stockings. I thought, holy fright, I wouldn't want to do the laundry here.

We'd bring our noontime lunch to work. We didn't know whether we were going to work at night or not. Bob might say, We're going to work late tonight.

That was okay.

Now, don't take off. Stay right here. You can have supper with us. There's always room at our table for two more. Just a really great guy.

Mary always cooked. She worked in the field and the potato house, too. I couldn't believe anybody could roll a barrel of potatoes like Mary could because she's not a big woman. A potato barrel weighs 165 pounds and she's rolling that like it's nothing.

I thought, Well, if she can do that, I can do that. Yeh, give me a break. You sure can. There's a trick to that, I'll tell you.

When we came in, we'd wash up. Mary was cooking. I was impressed because I had never seen this before. They kept a barrel of potatoes in the pantry. I mean, a barrel. A complete barrel of potatoes, and she would just peel the potatoes right there and cook them. You can imagine how many potatoes they would go through with a family that size. Unbelievable. I'd never seen that before. It sure was convenient for her.

Boy, I'll tell you, she's a good cook, too. They always ate well— potatoes, meat, or steak. She would cook it right up for you. It made no difference who was there. They are an amazing family. Whatever they had, they shared it.

At the end of the season we had a nice big meal and dance. The barn would be cleaned up. Mary would have everything set up for a big meal and we'd have a dance and Bob would have a band come in. They'd say, Just bring yourselves and have a good time. As always, they had plenty of food. Holy fright! There was no question of food. We did that every year. It was a lot of fun. That was a special time.

CHAPTER THIRTY-FOUR

John Eivers

I always felt like I was one of theirs in a way . . . I was closer to them than I was my own family.
    ~John Eivers

I was teaching at the time when I worked for Bob for several years during the fall harvest.

Bob's a pretty levelheaded person, takes things kind of easy. I very rarely saw him get upset or angry. You don't see him lose his temper very often. But I can think of one time when he lost it.

I drove truck under the harvester for Bob and he was always telling me, *Never* drive down the hill. Back down the hill. It's a good lesson to learn. Never drive down a hill.

We were on the Price Farm and I drove down the hill to turn around, rather than going up the hill and backing down, and then pulling up beside the harvester. And we kind of delayed quite a bit because of that, and that's the one time I saw Bob really lose his temper. I figured my days were gone on the farm there. He was quite upset because we had had a few other delays, too, before that.

On potato ground, you're digging in the middle of the field, and you have those two rows you can manipulate. On the end is a very narrow strip of land that you drive on. If you drive up the hill and back down, you can drive back into your row easily. I didn't. I drove down the hill and I couldn't get enough traction to back it up. It was early morning and the grass had dew on it. It was wet and we were just not going anywhere. He already told me not to do that. I thought I knew better, being a young whippersnapper. He probably told me why. He had said that was the way to do it and that was how he wanted me to do it.

It was a steep hill. Going down was quite a job, too. Trying to get turned around at the bottom—you had no place to turn around. If you picked up enough speed, you could lose a whole load of potatoes easily.

We ended up having to empty at least half of the load that I had on there. Yes, on the ground. He ran the harvester through again, so it wasn't that much of a chore, but Bob was very fussy about his potatoes. He didn't want them damaged in any way, and I kind of damaged a whole load of potatoes, which is quite a bit of money when you look at what you could potentially lose. That's the only time I saw him get upset. I didn't lose my job. He got over it. We all got over it.

Bob had a good reputation as a farmer and he would do anything to protect it. To show you the kind of person Bob is, I can remember one year we were shipping potatoes out overseas. The potatoes were loaded onto train cars and sent to Searsport to be loaded onto a ship. They got down there and the inspector was inspecting the cars. Several carloads were rejected. He wasn't going to let any of them in that line go. After Bob got word of that and we had worked from 6:30 in the morning until 3:00 in the afternoon, we then drove all the way to Searsport and worked half the night re-bagging all those potatoes. Drove all the way back and started again at 6:30 the next morning. That's the kind of guy he was. We got a chance to sleep a few hours in a motel. He wanted his reputation to stay untarnished and it didn't matter whether he was shipping them overseas or not. A lot of people didn't care.

I chummed with him and his wife and we went out some. He liked to dance and have a good time. I remember the barn dances at the Ashby farm.

I worked on the Ashby farm and I remember the barn fire. That was the largest barn in Aroostook County. I wasn't there but I worked for the Caribou Fire Department. I pulled standby in Presque Isle and it was quite a night to be out. It was just so icy and whatnot, they couldn't get the trucks up there. That's why it burned down. It was so windy that night; the electrical wires pulled away from the barn, hit one another and arced, causing a short circuit. Bob was upset at his son Roger. Everybody else got out of the house and Roger was sound asleep. They had a hard time waking him up.

John Eivers, Arthur Benner driving

Thirteen *is* a Lucky Number

Bob wanted everyone out of the house in case the fire went over to the house.

I used to kid him that he was in no man's land because he had a Caribou postal address, a Fort Fairfield phone number, and resided in Presque Isle.

During harvest time, if Bob wanted to work later at night, all the hands were invited in for supper. I remember sitting down at the table. There was like yelling up, Pass the potatoes, or something. There were 13 kids lined up right there, plus a few others.

Mary worked outside, too. I can tell you a few things about Mary. She was a good hard worker. She always had a smile on her face, a great person to know and be with. She rolled a barrel of potatoes with one hand up a 12-inch plank. Take it right up. A hundred and sixty-five pounds! There was a knack to it. I could roll one after a while. Mary was quiet, laid-back, and kept to herself, but she was not a shy person with people she knew. She likes to have a good time. She joked and held her own.

I was with Bob when he used barrels, and later the harvester. I remember coming down Sawyer Hill with his old International truck. He never did tell me that the brakes were a little weak, you know. I had a full load of barreled potatoes on there. Got down to the bottom and there's no place to go but right or left or straight into the field. I got down there and I didn't have any brakes. I was moving it, and went right, made it around the corner on two wheels. I think the whole load shifted to the left and I made it up to his father's place where we stored the potatoes. Bob was up there waiting for me.

Jeezum Crow, what did you do?

I went around the corner a little fast.

It looks that way. The load's over on the left.

We had to get something under that in order to loosen up the chains before we could drop it or I'd drop the whole load. The whole load was sitting to the left. I'll never forget that day. I said, Bob, you didn't tell me you had trucks with no brakes on them.

I never missed a day all the time I worked for him.

Bob is a wise person. If I had a problem I wouldn't hesitate to talk to him about it. He could analyze things without the fluff. He'd tell you just the way it is.

I had a time when I was driving for them and I was taking some medication. I would be driving down the field and, for no reason at all, start bawling my eyes out. I had no clue what was going on. Bob would tell me, You know, other people have it harder than you have. Don't be so down. Be a man about it.

Then later he asked me what I was taking for medication and said I ought to go back and see the doctor about that. I found out it was the medication that was the problem. It was a scare for me and it was nice to have a friend that you could call on. What he said had a lot of stock to it. I believed a lot of what he said.

Another time I fell through the floor of the gym at the high school while trying to get a set of films for teaching first aid. I split open my scalp, but I still went out to the farm, though, the next day. He'd ride me about that. Yeh, going to a first-aid class. Some first-aid instructor you must be—can't even tell where the hole is in the floor.

He trusted anybody. He'd give you all. Bob had a new Massey Ferguson tractor and he liked that tractor. This guy backed up into the front end of it. Kind of bent up the grill a little bit. I thought after getting a lashing about going down the hill the wrong way, this guy has had it, right? Didn't faze Bob in the least.

Well, we'll have to paint that up at the end of the season. It'll look like new again.

That's the way he was. Water flowed over the duck's back. If anybody did get hurt, Bob was the most caring person and would do anything to help them. Both Bob and Mary would help anybody.

I grew up in New York City. Big transition to here. I didn't know the first thing about farm equipment and machinery. I met Bob through working for Nason McGlinn. Bob needed some help and Nason didn't, so I went to work for Bob. I worked for Peter Campbell, too.

I think I learned a lot from Bob—some direction as to what I wanted to do. I learned a lot of patience from him. I was not a very patient person and working with him, somehow it seemed to rub off. I could see, Yeh, things always seem greener on the other side of the fence, but it's not always that way. There are always people who are worse off than us, no matter how bad things might seem.

Bob did a lot of different things. He's not the kind of person to sit around. He was quite an entrepreneur. I know that he and Mary sold Amway products. He wanted to open up a store and Amway wouldn't let him do that. It had to be door-to-door.

I know he started the Viking Sewing Center. He had quite a business for himself while he was farming. He always said, I can't get out of farming, though. I couldn't live if I didn't farm. That's how I feed my family.

I think when the day came when he could get out, he got out of it at the right time.

I knew Bob's father. John was a pretty stubborn gentleman. I remember having to haul potatoes and John was quite old then. He would come out and John wanted it done one way. You did it the way John wanted it done or not at all. There were no ifs, ands or buts about it. We used to store some in the little potato house on his farm. He was pretty obstinate. If John wanted to drive the truck back there, he was going to drive it back there, whether he could or not. He was going to. John was one of these: If he wanted to pull out, he owned the road. You get out of my way.

His brother Bill was the same way. They have that Campbell blood in them, and if they want to get stubborn, they can get stubborn.

Bob has always been an outgoing, outspoken person. This is his opinion; this is the way it is. If you don't like it, you didn't have to agree with it. You're entitled to your opinion; I'm entitled to mine. We used to get into quite a few discussions about teachers' salaries. I didn't agree with his opinion, naturally. And Bob liked to be the devil's advocate. So, if you said that book was white, he'd say it was black just to be obstinate.

There were discussions about town taxes and money. He claimed farmers were poor. I'd say farmers have got more money than they know what to do with. Neither one of us really believed what the other one was saying.

Bob lived pretty good on farming. He had a large family. They didn't have much when they first got married. I saw where they lived in that little house. The kids lived in the attic.

I was a young kid from New York City who was lucky to get stationed up here at Loring Air Force Base. That's how I would end up staying here. Twenty some-odd years later I married a local girl, so that wasn't what kept me here. It was families like Bob's that kept me here. I was like one of the McGlinn family. Bob treated me just as if I was one of his. I always felt like I was one of theirs in a way. I couldn't have been any closer. I was closer to them than I was to my own family.

People in families in New York are independent. Well, I learned here that you don't have to be independent. Families are families and you stay together and you work together and help each other out in times of need. That was probably the main reason that I stayed up here was because of the McGlinns and the Campbells. They welcomed me. They had a big impact on my life.

I laugh when I think of this. Being a driver's ed instructor, I always tell the kids to expect the unexpected.

I was driving the bulk truck and coming from the Price Farm back down toward John's. Mary was unloading us, working the back end of the truck as we dumped. She controlled the conveyor going into the barn and I controlled the conveyor on the truck, so you don't unload too many at a time and damage them. I was a little late getting there and Mary had been waiting around, so she decided to go up to the farm to bring us our lunches. I was coming down the road and I was moving it right along for a load of potatoes.

I don't know what Mary was thinking, but instead of turning up in the driveway, she turned and cut right across in front of me. I wasn't 30 feet from her. It scared the daylights out of me as well as it did her. I got there first. By the time she got herself back, she realized that she almost got herself killed that day. She backed out and come up with this grin on her face. I didn't say anything.

She said, I did something wrong, didn't I?

Mary, you sure did.

She said, But I won't tell Bob. We laughed about that.

She said, I could see the whites of your eyes. That's how close we were.

I don't know if Bob knows to this day. He probably does. We wound up talking about those kinds of things later on. And Mary probably wouldn't keep a secret from him. She had all this on her mind. Never gave it a thought. There was a driveway to the left and a driveway to the right, and she went to the one on the left.

I always tell my students if there are two choices, always go to the right so you don't cut across traffic.

Every year the Lions Club sponsored a Sportsmen's Show auction supper and they give out prizes. Bob invited me along. Bob had always won the prize for having the most number of kids. I can remember the year I went, he'd had the record for eight or ten years. He said, Ah, John, I'm going to get this prize. I've got the most number of kids.

It turned out there was somebody else that year who had one more than him. He lost out. He automatically assumed he was going to get it. We chuckled over that for a long time.

CHAPTER THIRTY-FIVE

Dana Allison

Most amazing to me, still, is how Bob and Mary were able to raise 13 children during a time when most couples have all they can do to support, guide, and direct only two or three children.

~Dana Allison

One day, about 20 years ago, I took my sewing machine into Bob and Mary Campbell's store to have it serviced. After telling Bob about what was amiss with the sewing machine, a FOR SALE sign in the store's window caught my eye as I left the store. Wheels churned on my way home. Jobs in Aroostook County, Maine, have never been plentiful. I had been looking for a job, but could not find one which I believed would satisfactorily utilize my abilities and talents. A day or two later I decided to buy out Bob Campbell. I had sales experiences from years before, and knew quite a bit about sewing, per se, from experience dating back to the time I was four years of age. I believed that this would be a good job opportunity for me to fill.

When I returned to Bob's store a couple of days later, Bob was very apologetic about not having gotten to my machine yet. He was quite surprised upon learning that I was more interested in buying him out. We made a deal, and the store was mine. Bob would stay on to do servicing and repairs to sewing machines, fill in as a sales clerk from time to time.

In Bob and Mary, both, I found a most gracious couple. Bob's knowledge of the sewing business and sense of humor made him an excellent mentor for me. Down through the years both Bob and Mary became fine friends whom I cherish. Their daughter, Roberta, who worked part-time for me, also became a fine friend. The parents' work ethic imparted to their daughter was a truly valuable asset to my enterprise.

Most amazing to me, still, is how Bob and Mary were able to raise 13 children during a time when most couples have all they can do to support, guide, and direct only two or three children. Others of their sons and daughters whom I met exhibited the same friendliness and graciousness of the parents. All had sparkling eyes, warm smiles, and every time we crossed paths there came the impression that we were long-time best friends.

One incident firmly implanted in my memory bank, related here, illustrates Bob's ability to meet a difficult situation. A couple came into the store to pick up their sewing machine, which Bob had serviced. The woman was tall, lanky, very skinny, a sallow complexion. Some of her teeth were missing, hair straight, in need of shampooing and styling. She seemed apprehensive, on the spot, fearful of the man with her. The man, also tall, lanky, had a well-developed muscular structure. His facial expression was sneering. He looked as if he were tightly wound, ready to spring at the slightest provocation. My impression was that he would give us much grief if that sewing machine they came to claim had not been repaired. I retrieved the machine, looked at the tag, and told the woman what Bob had found and repaired, stated the fees for Bob's work. My words of explanation, carefully chosen, were uttered with a lumpy throat. Bob, standing a few feet away, watched calmly, yet gave the impression that that man need not cause trouble; he defused the standoff resembling a confrontation between two bulls. Both of us heaved a great sigh of relief when that pair went out the door.

After a few years in business I decided to retire, and closed the store. Our friendship has continued on. Bob and Mary went into another retail business which I patronized when sewing supplies and sewing-machine repairs were needed. Each time we met Bob and Mary made me feel like a member of their family. We would catch up on our respective families' news, exchange stories about this and that, and have a grand time enjoying each other's company. Bob and Mary Campbell are a couple whom I admire, and enjoy knowing.

CHAPTER THIRTY-SIX

Ruth Anderson

*Mary is a remarkable mother. She knows there's enough love
to go around and she doesn't mind sharing her children.*
~*Ruth Anderson*

RUTH: I've met all of the Campbell children, but the two that I
love so much are Janet and Kim because they came to my house.
One of the teachers at Fort Fairfield High School called me up one
day and said, Would you like a couple of girls to clean your house?

I was all for that because it's such a big house.

The teacher said, I have two sisters and they're wonderful. And
so they came. Janet mows the lawn and still takes care of the flowers
here at my house. She thinks that she has a debt to pay to society.

Kim likes to read, so she read and read and read. Janet liked to
enjoy my company so when it was lunchtime, I'd say, Kim, put the
book away, we're going to talk.

I wanted her to talk because she's very smart. Mary, I think
she's the smartest of your children. That's what I think. I don't know
about you but I think she is. I'm a professor and I've worked with
children for a long, long time. Doesn't she speak beautifully now
with everybody? It's wonderful, but I don't take credit for that. I just
knew it was an important thing for her to do.

Kim, Ruth Anderson and Janet, 1993 (Drapes made by Mary)

She's very well built, tall and slim and pretty. She's not shy with me or her mother.

When I first found out that she was working at The Jade Palace restaurant, she said to me, I don't know if I'll ever get married.

I said, Look, you have a perfect place. Someday a man will come there, and he'll start talking to you. Then he'll come back another night, and he'll bring you flowers. Then he'll come another night, and he'll take you out to dinner. That's exactly what happened. And she married him—Kevin. Until Kim had her baby she was the most wonderful cleaner. I always told the girls that after they were done cleaning, to sit down and look around and see what they could see.

Kim said that she still does that. Her home is immaculate. And she and Kevin will still run errands for me. But compared to Janet, who is outgoing, yes, Kim's shy.

Janet talks constantly and she's happy. I have never seen her sad, ever, ever. She does a lot of things for me, running to get something out of the closet because it's hard for me. She'll do anything for me. She's trying to teach her children. She brings them with her and they watch what she does. Now they're taking my dog out.

———※◇※———

Someone reported Janet for taking time out to help people when she was delivering the mail. They sent a manager on the route with her. After all that, she was still twice as fast as anyone else. When she has a day off, they have to hire two people to do her mail route.

The Campbell children, they have picnics in the wintertime. Now, no other family that I know does that. And almost all of them show up and they go sleigh riding and they cook on the barbecue. That's amazing.

And they all like each other. That's what I like. Nothing ever mean. They never talk about each other. They really love each other.

Mary is a remarkable mother. She knows there's enough love to go around and she doesn't mind sharing her children. I give her all the credit in the world. And her husband, too. He's more precise and he expects them to behave, and [Mary doesn't] worry about that so much. He is strong and she is motherly and loving and it's a good combination. Her husband is a nice man. I like him very much.

When I was in a wheelchair, maybe we were both on crutches, he said, I'll race you.

He's a handsome man, and they are a lovely family.

I don't know how you did it, Mary, with 13 children. The girls told me that you had time to make clothes for those girls. How did you do that?

MARY: I used to do a lot at night and when they were having naps. I used to bake at night a lot, too.

RUTH: The girls have been very faithful to me. Usually when high school kids graduate from college, that's the end, but they have been faithful.

They have introduced me to all their sisters and brothers. I knew Michael, the one who lives in New Hampshire, the best of the boys. He is a lovely boy. Mary Nightingale could have married him a long time ago. But in the end, she married her high school sweetheart anyway. It's really quite remarkable how they all turned out.

The thing that I like is that they love each other and get along. That is very important in a family. They are a remarkable family from the mother and father right down through all the children.

CHAPTER THIRTY-SEVEN

Ruth and Art Mraz

The Campbells are dedicated to everything they are connected with—their church, their town, their business, and all that makes Fort Fairfield such a special place.
~Ruth and Art Mraz

If a national contest were held to locate one of the loveliest and most loving families in America, we think Mary and Bob Campbell and their brood would win hands down. No one could top the Campbells and their 13 beautiful and handsome offspring!

Mary and Bob sure have the secret to bringing up such a wonderful group of young people who have gone on to have happy, inspiring marriages, and children of their own. What an example they all have set to everyone who knows them.

The Campbells are dedicated to everything they are connected with—their church, their town, their business, and all that makes Fort Fairfield such a special place. They have certainly been at the forefront of a myriad of activities and organizations in the area.

Frontier Heritage, Fort Fairfield's Historical Society, has benefited from their dedication and sage advice. Their interest and volunteerism have been passed on to the next generations, and these individuals, especially Pat, Wayne, and family, have been a driving force in saving the

Society. They are fine examples to others in town who appreciate their loyal allegiance to this important endeavor.

We must comment on the great sense of humor that both Mary and Bob possess. Mary's bright smile is legendary and she sees the positive side of every situation. In spite of Bob's illness over the years, he always tries to look on the bright side.

We remember visiting him at the Van Buren Border View Rehab Center where he shared a room with another gentleman. This man delighted in being Bob's roommate because Bob provided the life spark that kept the man from being lonely and depressed. In fact, when offered a private room, the man declared he wouldn't move because he was having so much fun talking with Bob and his family, as well as other visitors.

Yes, the Campbell family members are a credit to our town, state, and nation. America needs more families like them. They provide the right example for others to follow. It is a pleasure for us to write our sentiments for the book and offer our heartfelt congratulations and affection to them as they continue to be the very special people they are.

CHAPTER THIRTY-EIGHT

Lynn Thibeau

*I still think it's quite an accomplishment to be able to name
all of Janet's brothers and sisters.*
  ~Lynn Thibeau

My first memory of Janet was in Mrs. Marshall's class in fifth grade. Mrs. Marshall was taking attendance and I heard her call the name Janet. I looked over to see who it was because I had never had a Janet in any of my classes before. From what I could tell, she seemed to be a nice person.

When the class ended and we all got up to change classrooms, Janet and I had our first encounter. I said to her, Ya know, my mother has a best friend named Janet.

I don't remember Janet's response (of course, what the heck is she supposed to say to that?), but it seems as if we have been friends ever since.

We live about three hours apart now, and life and distance have limited the frequency of our visits. But as it is with a true friend, we always pick right up where we left off from the last time we were together—laughing, sharing stories and dreams, and then saying goodbye with a hug.

When I think of Janet, the words that come to mind include:

honest, trustworthy, kind, caring, friendly, fun, solid values, grounded, very hardworking, bright, a strong heart and soul. And tall, too. She's much taller than I am.

Janet has always been a trusted friend. She is kind and friendly to everyone. She is solid in her beliefs, which makes her a very grounded person. She is wise about life, regarding everything from money to relationships. Her heart and soul are strong. I have seen her sad (which breaks my heart), but nothing ever gets her completely down. Even when she is hurt, she is still relatively upbeat and positive, and still gets through the day without much downtime. That may be due to the fact that she is such a hard worker and never slows down! Only once in a great while will I hear her say, I'm going to take a nap.

Janet is without a doubt a truly wonderful person, and I feel so fortunate to not only have her in my life, but also to be a part of her (and her family's) life.

I remember a handful of times when I had been at the Campbell house during one holiday or another, and there were so many people there! It was great! I come from a scrawny family of only four kids, about a third of the amount of Campbell kids.

And I still think it is quite an accomplishment to be able to name all of Janet's brothers and sisters. I think I can even name most of her nieces and nephews!

Regardless, these qualities that I have described about Janet most likely come from the fact that they are qualities of which the entire Campbell family is composed. And anyone who knows them would likely say the same.

It is a privilege to be able to contribute to this book, which recognizes and celebrates the spirit of this very special family.

CHAPTER THIRTY-NINE

The Liar's Club

I am impressed with Bob's independent spirit. After church,
Bob rides his wheelchair up Fort Hill, even in the rain.
                                    ~Dick Pelletier

On July 13, 2005 (this number 13 keeps popping up), as the
author of *Thirteen* is *a Lucky Number,* I, Trudy, was guest at the Fort
Fairfield Seniors Coffee Club—aka, The Liar's Club—which meets
for coffee every Wednesday at two p.m. at the Village Restaurant.

Permission granted, I was invited by Bob O'Brien (who isn't
old enough to be a member, but encounters the group often) to have
coffee with them. Bob thought some of the members might know
the Campbell family members and have stories to tell—true or not!

The club has been meeting for 15 years. They have lost three
members to death. I got the impression that one should be male, 70-
something, and be able to drink coffee in midafternoon. Membership
includes anyone who can stretch the truth.

Besides Bob O'Brien and me, those present included: Keith
Higgins, Luther McLaughlin, Ernie Ward, Don Gallagher, Preston
(Prep) Newcomb, Dick Pelletier, Roy Russell, and Charles Fowler.

Keith said, That Janet is a sweetheart. She carried mail the
whole time she carried two babies.

343

Thirteen *is* a Lucky Number

Ernie said, Janet is the best! When my wife was sick, she'd bring the newspaper right into the living room. They don't make 'em any better.

Don told about Sharon, the oldest of the thirteen Campbell children. She has worked at MFX [Maine Farmers Exchange] for 33 years. Some years ago in 1980, she had asked for time off to be with her new baby. Her boss told her to get a babysitter. She said she couldn't afford one. He said, Sorry.

She quit. Then he had to get her back because no one knew how to do her job. Besides her own four children, she was also babysitting her sister's children through digging. He doubled her pay so she could pay for a babysitter (after digging was over).

Dick said, I am impressed with Bob Campbell's independent spirit. After church, Bob rides his wheelchair up Fort Hill, even in the rain.

Roy remembered some of the children running the ice cream truck over at Loring Air Force Base. It helped put them through college. One would graduate and the next one would take it over.

Luther remembers when the Campbells won the Megabucks, that Bob didn't want to take all the money. Is this a lie? I asked myself.

Meeting adjourned until tomorrow.

~Trudy Chambers Price

Part IV
Vignettes

CHAPTER FORTY

Vignettes

One day we had a big group at the house to have pork chops. The pork chops got dumped outside. We just grabbed the hose and hosed them down and put them back on the grill and brought them in and never told anybody.

~Sharon

———◆———

I remember working for Roger and when he was irritated, he'd look at his watch, look back and forth, and tap on his watch.

~Jenny

———◆———

The Campbell family crossed the Caribou Bridge one Sunday morning on their way to the Holy Rosary Catholic Church, when someone in the car noticed that Jimmy was missing. It turned out that while they were getting ready for church, Jimmy had jumped down from the "stay-clean" bench, played in the plantings, and got dirty. He was sent to the bathroom to clean up again. Mary got busy rounding everyone up, and they drove off, leaving Jimmy in the bathroom. Mary and Bob thought that Grammy and Grampy Campbell who lived next door would notice him and look after him.

~Phil McNeal

———⟫·◆·⟪———

A group of us—Bob, Mary, Bob O'Brien, Pam, Kevin, and I—had gone to Karl's German Cuisine in Grand Falls one evening. When we came back across the Canadian border, we met Andy Coiley. After chatting a bit, he told us this story: After he had finished his Border Patrol [Homeland Security] training, he and a buddy flew on a Delta flight from Atlanta to Boston. Andy noticed Kim Campbell in the terminal, looking very pretty in her uniform. Thinking he would have some fun with his buddy, Andy bet him that he could get a hug from the pretty flight attendant. He walked over and greeted her. She reached over and gave him a hug. He proudly walked back and looked at his buddy, whose mouth was still wide open. Andy's buddy had lost his bet. What Andy had neglected to tell his buddy was that Kim had been his neighbor on Fort Hill Street in Fort Fairfield, Maine!

~Toni Phillips

———⟫·◆·⟪———

The only one born in the Ashby house was Kim. The oldest and youngest weren't born with the rest.

~Mary

———◆———

A lesson I learned growing up: Don't work for Dad!

~Joan

———◆———

I go back to the old philosophy that what we're doing today is not really right. I don't think anybody should be paid more than the President of the United States. And it's not right when they have all these sports people getting way, way, too much money; and show-people getting way too much money and not giving anything back. I think if they would stick to the family idea and all go to the ball games that their high schools have and get to know the players as well as they know the people who play on the Boston Red Sox, they'd enjoy it every bit as much and get in there for five dollars apiece or less, instead of this great big unreal $200 to take a family to a ball game. That's foolish. That's ridiculous. It's a rip-off! That's the way I see it.

There would be more done for a family to be together right in their own hometown. If they put their money in there, they would have better schools and better kids. A lot of things could be changed to enjoy it more because you can sweat, your heart could beat as fast for a good basketball, baseball, or football game near home. You don't do that when you pay the big money to go to these others.

~Bob

Thirteen *is* a Lucky Number

I don't worry about laws. That's why we have lawyers. One lawyer says one way, the other lawyer says the other way. How am I supposed to interpret it? I interpret the law the way I want. If I say I'm going to do something, I'm going to do it. I don't care what other people think or what the law says.

~Bob

Robert, it's Wayne.

I'm writing to you about your daughters and the wonderful basketball they played at Fort Fairfield. I remember three of them playing and being the most determined players I had ever seen. I'm not so sure that at one point I remember four Campbells in a game. I also remember that it was a nightmare remembering all the first names. They gave me fits keeping it all straight. In retrospect, I had a lot of twins who played over the years, but I think the Campbell girls, as I called them, were the only three or four sisters who played on a team at one time.

They were something, and good-looking, too.

~Wayne Knight, radio announcer

Bob, all I can say is that you married the right sister because one of the other three would have gone for a swim with cement shoes on, a long time ago.

50th Wedding Anniversary party, February 5, 2006
b: Dave, Gary, Michael, Jim
m: Sharon, Roberta, Barb, Pat, Joan, Kim, Janet
f: Bob and Mary

On another note, your endless generosity has always amazed me. After Pudge's graveside service, you and Mary brought all the food in for brunch afterwards. When I offered to pay, you said, I don't charge anyone else, why should I charge you?

The philosophy that you instilled in your family is remarkable—you receive, you give back.

Thank you, Bob, for all you have done for us, and the community.

~Toni

Thirteen *is* a Lucky Number

━━◆━━

I remember when Dave got run over by a truck. They had trimmed the brushes along the line fences and were having a big bonfire. They had a marshmallow roast. They were playing hide-and-seek in the oats. Robert's father went to move the truck, and Dave was hiding under the truck. He laid right down and went between the wheels. It scared him but it didn't hurt him.

~Mary

━━◆━━

Mary [Nightingale] sang the National Anthem at the tournament, with no music. That was a first. That was when the girls were in the tournament. She can belt out "New York, New York," like anything. She sings at weddings.

Sherrill and Daniel are good singers, too. So is Brad, but he's shy and won't sing in public. He used to sing in the choir in church but when he got older, he didn't do it anymore. Danny was Mr. Caribou. He's very good on the stage. Sherrill also plays guitar. Sherrill and Mary were both beauty queens. Sherrill was Miss Caribou and Mary was Miss Southern Aroostook and Miss Maine.

~Mary

━━◆━━

When the kids talk about the little house and how they can't believe they all fit in there—that's because they were small. That's what they don't understand. One of the bedrooms downstairs had three cribs in it. Ten by ten, I think. It's the same thing with the car. How did we all fit in the car? Well, we probably had five or six in the backseat. I really don't know how they all did fit in the car, though. Good thing there were no seat belt laws then.

~Mary

Them washing machines were quite something. About the only washing machines we had—I used to go to Maine Public Service in Caribou. They'd get trade-ins. I'd go in and pick up their trade-ins. Sometimes they'd have two or three and I'd bring them home and put them together and get one working. I got this here what they called "easy" washing machine. It spun and spun. We had to tie that down with a chain. It'd get going and pull the cord right out of the socket. After we moved to the Ashby farm we bought our first new one.

~Bob

If we decided to go somewhere one night we packed and we went in the morning. We never set ourselves to a schedule. Never rented a hotel ahead of time, just drive wherever we were going, stop where we were and go in. And go down the road. See something; take off on a side road. I see somebody doing something, I'd get out and climb up on the tractor with them and ride on the combine. Went through Georgia. There was a good old farmer out there. He seemed to be pretty busy, didn't hardly want to talk. I told him I was a potato farmer. Then I was there half the day. I'd never seen cotton before.

~Bob

Thirteen *is* a Lucky Number

You could sit down with each of the kids separately, and they could be talking about the same thing, and each one will have a different story, even if they all had been there at the same time. It's neither right or wrong, it's the way each one sees it.

~Bob

About the Author

Trudy Chambers Price was born in the Aroostook County town of Island Falls, Maine, and grew up in Caribou. Every fall from the ages of 10 to 18, she picked potatoes to earn money to buy her own clothes. On her record day she picked 100 barrels of potatoes (because her boyfriend pulled the tops).

Trudy graduated from Caribou High School in 1958 and from the University of Maine at Orono in 1962. For 23 years she was a partner on Craneland Farm in Knox, Maine, where she and her husband Ron, bred and milked Registered Holsteins. Their two sons, Kyle and Travis, grew up on the farm.

Trudy was first published at the age of nine, when her mother sent her poem and her drawing to *JACK and JILL* magazine.

She lives in Brunswick and works part-time for Islandport Press and Bath Book Shop.

She is the author of *The Cows are Out! Two Decades on a Maine Dairy Farm*.